Designing a distributed processing system

Designing a distributed processing system

HAMISH DONALDSON

A HALSTED PRESS BOOK

JOHN WILEY & SONS
New York – Toronto

English language edition, except USA and Canada published by
Associated Business Press, an imprint of
Associated Business Programmes Ltd
Ludgate House
107–111 Fleet Street
London EC4A 2AB

Published in USA and Canada by
Halsted Press, a division of John Wiley & Sons Inc
New York

First published 1979

Library of Congress Cataloging in Publication Data

Donaldson, Hamish
    Designing a distributed processing system

    1. Electronic data processing—Distributed processing. 2. Business—Data processing.
I. Title
QA76.9   D5D66   001.6′4   79–22523

ISBN 0 470 26889 1

© Copyright Hamish Donaldson 1979

Typeset by Photo-graphics, Honiton, Devon
Printed and bound in Great Britain by
Biddles Ltd, Guildford and King's Lynn

Contents

ACKNOWLEDGEMENT   viii

PREFACE   ix

CHAPTER 1   BACKGROUND TO DISTRIBUTED   1
PROCESSING

Cost trends
Analysing the cost trends
Pressures for distributing computer
applications
Two approaches to distributed processing
Summary

CHAPTER 2   IDENTIFYING THE BUSINESS NEED   23
AND ORGANISATIONAL IMPACT OF
DISTRIBUTED SYSTEMS

Understanding operating needs
Understanding management information
requirements
Organisational implications
Siting the VDUs
Summary

CHAPTER 3   DECIDING THE FILE STRATEGY   40

Constraints of information flow
Guidelines for deciding the file strategy
Organisational constraints
Summary

CHAPTER 4   COMMUNICATIONS NETWORKS   54

               2780 point-to-point communications
               Asynchronous transmission
               Using interactive VDUs
               Communications networks
               Summary of design implications

CHAPTER 5   FILE ACCESS METHODS   77

               Distributed files
               Transaction processing considerations
               Data analysis and file design
               File access methods
               Summary

CHAPTER 6   DECIDING THE HARDWARE STRATEGY   107

               Hardware overview
               Operating systems overview
               Essential basic software
               Choice of programming language
               Custom built hardware
               Choice of hardware

CHAPTER 7   WORKFLOW DESIGN   129

               Office environment
               Work posture
               Flow of work
               VDUs and screen design
               Security of access
               Training and supervision
               Special purpose terminals
               Summary

CHAPTER 8   DECIDING THE PROGRAMMING   153
               STRATEGY

               On-line program design
               Examples of program suites
               Building the software functions
               Using standard packages
               Summary

CHAPTER 9   PERFORMANCE CHARACTERISTICS   171

Queuing principles
Bottleneck areas
Summary

CHAPTER 10   RELIABILITY, SECURITY AND   185
               CONTROL

Reliability and availability
System recovery
Checklist of system controls
Security and privacy
Precautions against physical risks
Disaster control procedures
Summary

CHAPTER 11   OPERATIONAL RUNNING   207

Systems/operations interface
Site preparation
Operating standards and procedures
Training and post-implementation support
Summary

CHAPTER 12   CONTROLLING SYSTEMS DEVELOP—   218
               MENT

Structuring project responsibilities
Choosing the project manager
Stages of system development
Management style

SELECT BIBLIOGRAPHY   227

INDEX   230

Acknowledgement

We installed our first distributed system in Hill Samuel in 1974. In the five years that have elapsed we have replaced all the batch systems and improved the service to our users out of all recognition. Our distributed processing policies evolved after studying the experience of others and relating it to our own situation, and after a great deal of internal discussion. The major contributions were made by Archie Reid and his projects staff, Roger Moore and his operations team, and John Sharp and John Bray on the technical side. Michael Scott Morton of MIT provided external stimulus and counsel. Their collective contribution to the Hill Samuel systems and this book is considerable.

Preface

There is always a risk with a specialist that he has a solution which he is determined to fit to your problem. In a rapidly changing technology like data-processing, where general solutions take several years to mature, there is the ever present danger that the problem being solved has gone away by the time the solution is ready.

Distributed processing as a concept is likely to be permanent for two main reasons. As defined in this book it is oriented to putting computer power where the business needs it (it is problem-oriented and not solution-oriented); the philosophy is also consistent with the tumbling cost of hardware and the increasing cost of software.

The structure of the book is shown in Figure 1. Starting with a chapter to orientate the reader it goes on to cover all aspects in the design of a distributed system. The main purpose is to help systems designers to develop sound systems, using today's technology, that will serve their organisations into the late 1980s.

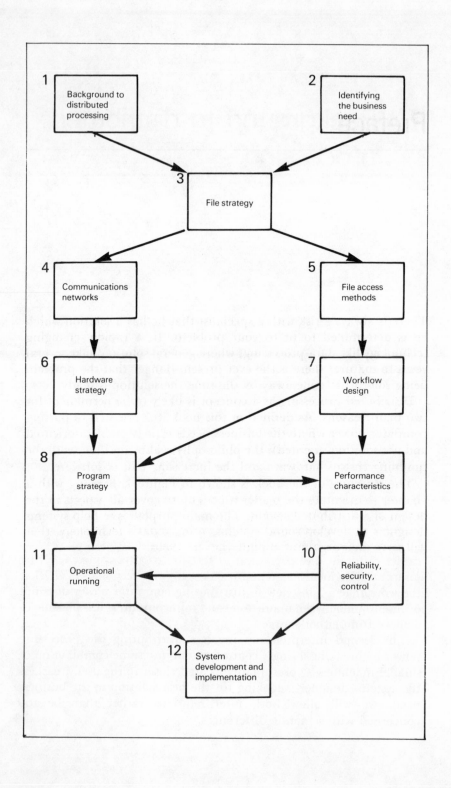

1 Background to distributed processing

Distributed processing as a topic has come to the forefront of systems thinking in the last few years. When computers were first introduced they were relatively expensive and untried. Business organisations had little alternative to installing centralised systems — whatever the ethos of the organisation.

The picture today is very different. The costs are no longer clearly in favour of the large central computer, more experienced computer users are not prepared to accept priority conflicts, and on-line systems are no technical novelty. Pressures from users are forcing a greater distribution of processing power to where the problems are.

Distributed processing, then, can be defined as 'putting computer power where the people and problems are' — a definition which has a business rather than a technical focus. This definition allows two rather different interpretations of distributed processing. The first interpretation means a greater use of computer terminals (VDUs) at the work place. This view of distributing computer power does not differentiate between mainframe and minicomputer; it is possible to achieve from either source.

The second interpretation involves distributing the processing power by breaking a single central system into some combination of smaller machines — presumably located closer to the user areas. As the systems designer is looking for the best solution to the business need, we will allow both interpretations rather than be too concerned with semantic differences.

What can be distributed: management view

Ask top managers what can be distributed and they will focus on the decision and control processes associated with:

— what gets built (management decision);
— how it gets built (systems analysts and programmers);
— who runs it (operators).

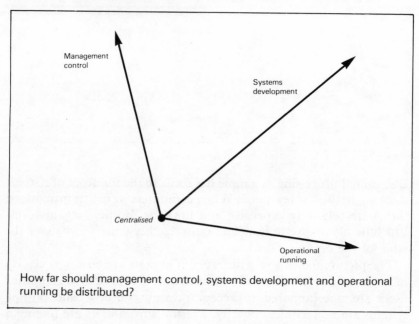

How far should management control, systems development and operational running be distributed?

Figure 1.1 Management view of distributed processing

When the computer pendulum was pointing towards *centralised* systems the decisions were easy. Well, only fairly easy, as it turned out that developing satisfactory systems, remote from the end-user, is quite difficult. All too often they did not really meet his needs, were cumbersome and unwieldy. In many organisations reaction set in and the pendulum swung towards *decentralised* systems. Again it was clear where the decisions were going to be made.

Even if decentralisation had its dangers (lack of central quality control, potentially higher cost, unstructured development in a corporate sense), it was likely to be no worse than systems which did not meet short-term needs and never seemed to realise longer-term goals either. And at least functional managers now had responsibility and authority.

What then is the difference between decentralised systems and distributed systems? Decentralisation implies delegation of authority to functional sub-units, retaining little more than a liaison role in the centre. There is thus no choice but a local operation. Distribution, on the other hand, implies that there is central control but that a positive decision has been made to distribute one or more of the operational running, systems development and management control functions.

Technological advances have allowed the pendulum to return closer to centre and today the pressures seem to be towards local responsibility for day-to-day operations and central responsibility for systems development. Responsibility for deciding what gets built is not so clear and will tend to vary more than the others with the type of organisation and the personalities involved.

What can be distributed: technical view

Ask technicians what can be distributed and they will focus on the location and interdependence of:

— processing power;
— data files;
— communications networks.

The rapid cost reduction in processing power over the last few years has transformed the problem of the systems designer. In the 1960s there were undeniable economies of scale and the idea of a processor for a small division was unthinkable. Today it is possible to purchase processing power economically from a one-VDU system up to systems with 100 VDUs or more. The systems designer can now concentrate on where he would like to locate the processing power, confident that there will be a cost-effective technical solution.

The location of data files is altogether a more difficult problem. While it is technically feasible to locate data files anywhere in the organisation, they are likely to be used in a variety of different applications with conflicting demands — in terms of response time, transaction volume and type of transaction. In fact, location of the data files is the major design problem — and guidelines for their location are set out in Chapter 3.

Communications networks are required to link together the distributed processors and data files. Simple point-to-point communications have existed for some time and are well understood. In Chapter 4 we examine some of the newer approaches to data transmission and the steps to be taken to ensure that today's designs will be compatible with future developments.

Cost trends

Most authorities are agreed that there is unlikely to be a single best policy for distributed processing or computing within an organisation. The more common computer alternatives are categorised below:

— central computer run in batch mode;
— remote job entry to central computer;
— VDUs linked to central computer (e.g. transaction processing or time-sharing);
— personal computer (one terminal with, say, a memory of 64k bytes, 2M bytes disc and good basic software);
— local stand-alone computers (with several terminals);
— local stand-alone computers with dial-up access to central computer;
— network of computers.

We shall now examine the various costs that make up a computer system and identify the trends over the last ten years. This will enable us to forecast the way costs will influence the popularity of the seven alternatives above, over the next five years.

Computer operations costs (£'000s p.a.)				
	Mainframe		Minis	
	1977/78	1978/79	1977/78	1978/79
Hardware depreciation	130	130	18	18
Operations staff	115	133	5	7
Accommodation	110	120	6	7
Maintenance	50	55	7	7
Consumables	50	54	3	4
Transmission	10	11	3	3
	465	503	42	46

Figure 1.2   Breakdown of computer operation costs

Figure 1.2 shows the budgeted costs for a mainframe computer (Honeywell 66) and a local small computer (PDP-11/45) in one installation in the financial years 1978/79 and 1979/80. Both computers are capable of five common ways of working using high level languages:

— batch processing;
— remote job entry;
— transaction processing on-line;
— time-sharing;
— program development on-line.

There are no data preparation costs included with either system, nor the cost of analysts and programmers.

There do seem to be a great number of mainframe operating staff and a breakdown is shown in Figure 1.3. Some of the number are due to three-shift working, there are others there because the mainframe is located in its own building; the centre also provides a back-up service to the minicomputer sites.

Mainframe operations staff:		
	1 ½	Operations manager and secretary
	1	Chief operator
	3	Shift leaders
	7	Operators (including mini-support)
	3	Planning and control
	2	Guillotine and decollating on shift
	1	Assistant manager administration
	1	Driver
	2	Building/air conditioning/ maintenance/security
	1 ½	Statistics/purchasing/accounts
		TOTAL: 23
Mini operations staff:	2	people, half time

Figure 1.3 Breakdown of mainframe operators

The minicomputer operations staff is based on two people half time. If an on-line system is to be operational during the whole working day, it needs to be brought up before the start of normal working hours. Similarly an operator is required to stay late and secure the system following the end of daily operation. An effective way of covering this extended hours working is for two members of the staff to alternate early and late working. Probably they will not be operating the minicomputer full time during the day and will be able to undertake other duties within the department as well.

In addition to the cost elements shown in Figure 1.2 there are two substantial cost areas which we will consider separately:

— cost of data input;
— cost of systems analysts and programmers.

The cost will be analysed in terms of UK£ with no correction for inflation. It is not intended that the cost forecasts should be precisely correct — more that they should indicate likely trends. The analysis has been done at a time of considerable inflation and a useful backcloth is the change in the UK cost of living index over the period covered (January 1962 was 100).

January	1970	1971	1972	1973	1974	1975	1976	1977	1978	1979
Index	135	147	159	171	192	230	284	331	364	397
1979 as 100	34	37	40	43	48	58	72	83	92	100

Cost of staff

The Computer Economics survey of computer staff salaries in the UK gives the figures in Figure 1.4. Figure 1.5 shows these normalised average staff salaries plotted against time as well as the cost of living index. *Taking a fairly optimistic view of inflation, staff costs* (salary, insurance, pension, expenses) *in five years' time will be nearly double those of today.* A logarithmic scale has been used on the assumption that costs tend to increase or decrease at a constant rate.

	National average basic salaries (£)			
	1968	1972	1976	1979
Job 01 DP manager	3225	5128	8209	10836
	(30)	(47)	(76)	(100)
Job 04 Systems analyst	1662	2490	4286	5582
	(30)	(45)	(77)	(100)
Job 13 Computer operator	957	1406	2537	3385
	(28)	(42)	(75)	(100)
Average	(29)	(44)	(76)	(100)

Figure 1.4   Average UK computer staff salaries

Hardware costs

To arrive at the overall trend in hardware costs, the computer components have been considered in three groups:

1. CPU and memory (about one-third of the cost at today's prices).
2. Disc storage (about one quarter).
3. Remaining peripherals and essential software.

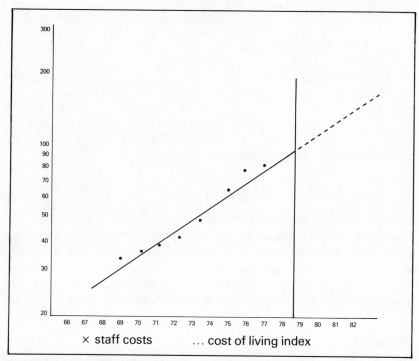

Figure 1.5 Staff salaries and cost of living index plotted against time

An analysis of figures provided by IBM, Honeywell and DEC suggests that over the last ten years:

— CPU and memory has reduced in value by a factor of 5;
— disc storage has reduced in price by a factor of 4;
— remaining costs have stayed about the same.

A direct comparison of price lists shows that the cost of CPU and memory has come down by a factor of 10 rather than the 5 above; but with more memory come bigger operating systems and less efficient languages, so for our purposes the lower factor seems more relevant. We are not looking at the cost of raw power, we are looking at the cost of readily usable power.

Applying the various factors, we see that a typical computer costing 100 units today would have cost about 300 units ten years ago.

	Current cost	Cost 10 years ago	
CPU and memory	33	165	(×5)
Discs	25	100	(×4)
Remainder	42	42	(×1)
	100	307	

From these figures, we can forecast that *hardware costs will approximately halve over the next five years.*

Accommodation and consumables

Accommodation costs include rent, rates, building maintenance, furniture, office equipment and telephones, security guards and other office-related expenses. Consumables include electricity, print ribbons, tapes, discs and stationery. The majority of these items are likely to be most influenced by the cost of living index and are therefore likely to double in cost over the next five years.

Hardware maintenance

The cost of hardware maintenance is influenced by three trends:

1. The cost of engineers is increasing, more or less in line with other staff.
2. The reliability of hardware is improving (particularly discs and solid state components).
3. The value of hardware being purchased does not seem to reduce, even if its cost performance is improved.

While maintenance costs increase each year for a given configuration, there has been little or no long-term increase for a given amount of power. We predict therefore that hardware maintenance costs will remain at about current levels — the staff cost increases being balanced by hardware cost reductions. In five years' time this means maintenance will have increased from 8 to 9 per cent per annum of hardware cost to 15 to 20 per cent.

Data transmission costs

The cost of telephone calls in the UK rose sharply between 1974 and 1976 but has not risen since. Figure 1.6 shows the way the standard rate for dialled calls has varied.

	1971 (Feb) time for 1p	norm	1974 (Sep) time for 1.5p	norm	1976 (Nov) time for 3p	norm	1979 (Jan) time for 3p
Local calls	6m	17	3m	50	3m	100	3m
Up to 35 miles	30s	50	48s	53	45s	100	45s
Up to 50 miles	15s	33	15s	50	15s	100	15s
Over 50 miles	10s	50	15s	50	15s	100	15s
Average		37.5		51.0		100	

Figure 1.6   Changing rates for standard telephone calls

In April 1975 the Tariff T (speech-type private lines) was increased by about 40 per cent (from 71 in 1975 to 100 today). These points are plotted on Figure 1.7 with the other trends. Line costs are forecast to more than double over the next five years. Note however that sending a magnetic tape by taxi is also data transmission.

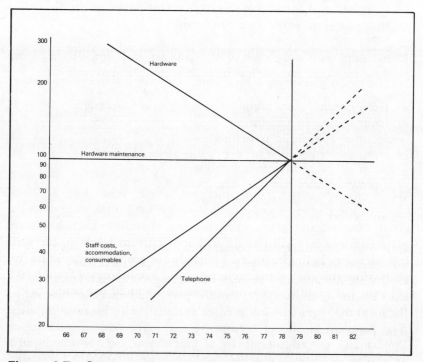

Figure 1.7   Cost trends over the last ten years projected forward for the next five years

It is tempting to think that higher transmission speeds reduce data-transmission costs. In practice the lower unit cost is not likely to be reflected in cost savings. The reason is that higher speeds can only be achieved at the present time using leased lines — where the cost is fixed irrespective of traffic.

Cost of data input

The major difference between batch and on-line systems is the method of input. In principle, an on-line system allows the clerk to work with the computer from original documents or perhaps from no documents at all (for example telephone sales). With a batch system, however, a number of additional steps are introduced:

— unnecessary coding and possibly transcription;
— batching and add-listing;
— punching;
— verifying;
— computer input;
— recycling and correction of errors (error prone in itself);
— re-input — so processing can begin.

These steps add only cost to the process and are all the worse because the work has to flow in such a complicated way:

— from original work station to coding and batching;
— from coding to add-listing;
— from add-listing to punching;
— from punching to verifying, with errors recycled;
— from verifying to computer room;
— from computer room to data control;
— from data control recycle errors;
— and so on.

It is not surprising that computers have got into disrepute if documents have to be subjected to this sort of paperchase. There are clearly significant staff savings in putting computer power at the work station — quite apart from the potential benefits of motivating the local manager who has greater authority with his responsibility. The problem is one of measuring the extra cost of data input. Empirically, the additional cost of batch input over on-line input is at least twice the staff cost required to operate the batch computer. So if the batch work requires ten operations staff there are twenty or more additional staff in the user departments or punch rooms who could be saved in a move to an on-line system. The cost of this staff is also likely to double in the next five years.

Systems analysts and programmers

There is not sufficient evidence to build a complete picture, but we do not see that a shift to distributed processors will have much impact on the numbers of systems analysts and programmers. Comparing on-line systems with batch (and assuming both have well-proven and suitable operating systems) we have found that:

1. On-line systems take longer to systems test, but are quicker to implement (because they are more like existing procedures) and are robust in operation (fewer residual errors).
2. On-line systems contain more programs, but they tend to be simpler programs.
3. On-line systems have additional security and recovery requirements but programs are developed faster interactively.

We have not detected much change either in the jobs of systems analysts and programmers. Systems analysts are more easily able to tailor local systems to local needs and if there seems to be unnecessary duplication they lose little or no time as a result (presumably because of the learning curve effect). Systems designers and programmers, of course, have to learn some new skills. For example, the critical factor in achieving fast response with an on-line system tends to be the disc. Disc space tends to be less critical than disc accesses (so combine records and avoid chaining); CPU cycles are usually less critical than program size (large programs take longer to swap).

   All in all we doubt whether user managers will get better at specifying their requirements because the computer moves closer — so we still need analysts. We also doubt whether software packages will be any more acceptable because the computer moves closer — so we still need programmers. And probably in about the same numbers, too.

Analysing the cost trends

The table in Figure 1.8 summarises our forecast of the cost trends over the next five years (in relative importance for current configurations). Given these cost trends we can see that the pressure will be to increase the amount of hardware in use if it means the other components can be reduced.

Cost of data input (batch)	double
Hardware	halve
Cost of operations staff	double
Accommodation	double
Hardware maintenance	double relative to hardware
Consumables	double
Telephone line costs	more than double

Figure 1.8   Forecast of cost trends over the next five years

We can now forecast the impact of the cost trends on the seven computer alternatives described earlier:

1. *Central computer run in batch mode:* the trend is *against* because of the escalating costs of data input, operations staff and accommodation.
2. *Remote job entry to central computer:* the trend is *against* because of the escalating costs of data input, operations staff, accommodation and line costs.
3. *On-line access to central computer:* the trend is more *slowly against* because data input costs are saved, operations costs can be contained, against which line costs for individual users could quickly become relatively high for geographically dispersed access. This solution will be cost effective for some time to come.
4. *Personal computer:* the trend is *strongly for* as virtually all the escalating costs are removed. In five years' time the personal computer with fast CPU, at least 64k bytes memory, 2M bytes disc, terminal and good software is likely to cost £5000-£6000 (£2500-£3000 at today's prices).
5. *Local stand-alone computers* where several terminals need to access one file (e.g. order entry): the trend is *strongly for,* as again virtually all the escalating costs are removed. Small local machines (PDP-11/34 size) can be run by part-time operators, accommodation requirements are marginal (unlike the central mainframe where they are very real) and even the use of consumables is reduced.
6. *Local stand-alone computers with dial-up access* to central computer: the trend is *strongly for* as again virtually all the

escalating costs are removed. There is no doubt that most organisations need to collect information for central processing and this is a way of achieving that result while containing increasing line costs.

7. *Network of computers:* the trend is *not clear*. With the exception of communication lines, the escalating costs can again be removed. While line costs are not necessarily a high proportion of total costs, networks are relatively new and potentially add costs because of complexity and risk. The short-term trend is therefore against, the long-term trend uncertain.

Summary of cost trends

In summary the cost trends are against:

— central batch computers;
— remote job entry computers.

The cost trends are in favour of:

— personal computers;
— local stand-alone on-line computers;
— local computer with dial-up access to the centres.

The cost trends are less clear for:

— on-line access to central computers (against in the long term);
— networks of computers (against in the short term).

If these are the cost trends it suggests that future computers will move towards the architecture of Figure 1.9.

This design exploits the advantages of the micro and improves throughput by limiting the job of the central machine to file management. Application programs are down-line loaded into the microcomputers (or maybe stored already in read only memory). The file management computer carries out queuing of disc accesses (maybe with some optimisation), and at a simple level carries out the file reading and writing. It will also contain the file access software up to a full database management system. It also carries out sorting, archiving to tape and printing (all of which are forms of file management).

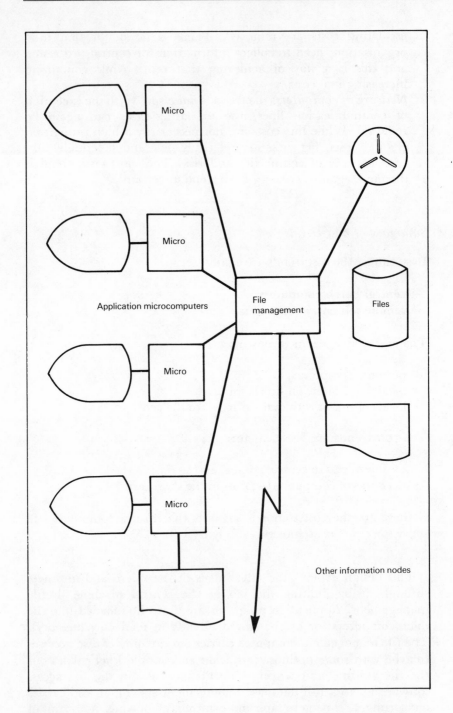

Figure 1.9   A future computer architecture

Pressures for distributing computer applications

Cost trends are not the only decision criteria. Other arguments in favour of distributed computing fall into the following broad categories: helping the business to realise its goals, helping cost/performance in the business, providing sound business systems and improving computer systems' cost/performance.

Improved systems development

— duplication of costs can be avoided in developing common applications;
— staff have career development opportunities within management services;
— smaller divisions can look to the centre for support;
— advantages of equipment standardisation;
— easier to apply systems' design quality control.

Improved business efficiency

— greater flexibility for incremental growth;
— reduced systems complexity;
— direct profit and loss accountability with responsibility;
— avoidance of 'central overheads' and problems of cost recovery;
— scheduling of priorities under local control.

Improved computer effectiveness

— more rapid response to local situations;
— less rigid solutions to business problems;
— less risk of development failure;
— less risk of operational running failure;
— easier to limit and recover from failure.

Improved computer efficiency

— greater throughput by parallel working of multiple computers;
— hardware can be 'application tailored';
— reduced application development time and cost;
— reduced data communication costs;
— fewer skilled staff required to support systems software.

Centralisation

There are other arguments, however, in favour of retaining a degree of centralisation:

Improved systems development

— duplication of costs can be avoided in developing common applications;
— staff have career development opportunities within management services;
— smaller divisions can look to the centre for support;
— advantages of equipment standardisation;
— easier to apply systems design quality control.

Other arguments:

— a need to share data files leads to greater centralisation;
— centralisation avoids problems of data duplication and synchronisation;
— local sites are freed from the responsibility of managing their own centre — and of shift working particularly;
— security and recovery can be kept under tighter control;
— small users can have access to central expertise;
— current investment in centralised systems makes change difficult;
— all organisations tend to have a need for some processing at the centre.

There are two messages which stand out from these arguments:

— business considerations are now significantly more important than technical considerations in the provision of processing power;
— central control of systems development is still desirable.

Business needs should dominate technical solutions

Cost trends and business arguments favour putting computer power where the people and problems are. Only a few years ago systems designers were constrained to look at business problems with a central batch solution in mind. It is now possible to concentrate on organising computers to match the business organisation — confident that a cost-effective technical realisation can be achieved.

Retain central control of systems development

The arguments in favour of central control of systems development are very powerful. The arguments *against* come down to:

— a desire for local control of systems development;
— resistance to paying an economic rate for central staff.

The first of these arguments is a throwback to the bad old days of amateur DP departments. There is nothing in a centrally controlled systems department to prevent local managers taking responsibility for their own systems. They can have the best of both worlds: responsibility for local development together with central quality control.

Small business computers may simplify applications development but the familiar rules must be followed:

— decide what you want to do first;
— design and review the solution carefully;
— specify in detail before programming starts;
— system test exhaustively before going live.

The design rules are not difficult, but they are very easy to get wrong; slow response is a continuing embarrassment and all too visible. The thought of going back to learning by frequent (distributed) mistakes does not bear thinking about. Happily there is also the possibility that controlling their own computer will remove some of the inhibitions of the user manager and cause the systems analyst to identify the solution more closely with the need it is now so clearly there to satisfy.

Resistance to paying an economic rate for central staff can be overcome in a number of ways. One is to charge staff out at their marginal employment cost — i.e. at the same rate as if the person was on the user's staff. Such an arrangement assumes that the management of the DP department, systems accommodation, etc. are acceptable as central overheads.

Moving back to operations staff, it is likely that there will be a continuing need for some central computer facility as central systems require a central computer. Such a situation is doubly satisfactory. We have observed that user departments can run their minicomputers with very little outside help — but they run them better if they are well trained and supported by a competent central operations staff.

In summary, a degree of centralised control is desirable, provided it is not remote from user managers. In large organisations some subdivision will be required to avoid the centre becoming too unwieldy.

Two approaches to distributed processing

Distributed processing can be achieved in a number of ways. One approach is to create a hierarchical network based on existing mainframe computers. A second approach is to place greater emphasis on stand-alone minicomputers.

The mainframe approach is illustrated in Figure 1.10 for an organisation with a head office, regional offices and a number of depots. In this example the main files are held at the regions for the daily work. Additional accounting and statistical files are held at head office and the remote job entry (RJE) link is sufficient for the purpose. The lines to the head office are shown as dial-up lines as the traffic volume is low and the lengthy connect time (fifteen seconds or so) is not a handicap.

If there is a hierarchical organisation structure it follows that a common programming language between processing levels would be a considerable advantage. Programming applications in one language to run on different sizes of machine gives the system designer the maximum flexibility in the development of his network. This mainframe approach is particularly suited to organisations with a tradition of centralisation, to those where a central database is essential to the business and to those where it is not possible to identify local stand-alone applications. It is also easier to operate remote sites if the data files are held centrally — avoiding problems of security and control.

The stand-alone approach to distributed processing is illustrated in Figure 1.11 — again for an organisation with a head office, regional offices and depots. As before, the host computer at head office may communicate with regional computers using remote job entry on dial-up lines. The difference lies in making the depot machines more powerful (with their own disc storage for data files) but only loosely connected to the regional computers. Perhaps the region is based at one of the depots so two machines there are side by side (providing a degree of back-up to each other and to the depots). In many cases the stand-alone approach will be practical (because depot applications are different from regional office applications) and will be preferred because of greater simplicity and higher throughput capacity.

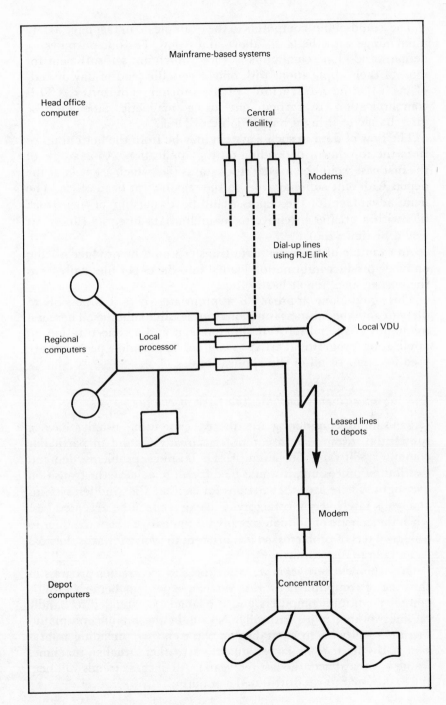

Figure 1.10   A hierarchical network

The 'stand-alone' computers in the example do in fact have a data interchange with the levels above and below. For our purposes we define stand-alone computers as those which are self-sufficient for most of their applications with only a periodic (end-of-day or end-of-cycle) communication with another computer. This communication is carried out using magnetic tape or disc interchange or using a remote job entry link.

The flow of data in such a system may be from the bottom up or from the top down, depending on the application. An example of the first case would be master stock status files which are held at the depots with only summary files in the region or at head office. The main advantage for the depots would be 'ownership' of their stock files with a greater incentive to maintain data integrity (line costs would be down too).

An example of top-down data transfer would be product pricing and new product information loaded into the depot files daily from the master stock file at head office.

This stand-alone approach is appropriate where it is possible to disaggregate the business functions into sensible subunits. There is a minimum of special software development and a concentration on application programs. Perhaps standard application packages are used for some or all of the applications.

Existing investments will slow the pace of change

Organisations considering distributed computing usually have a substantial investment in computers already — and in particular computer software. So, even if the business problems demand distributed processing, it would be difficult to achieve the transition overnight. There are other reasons for caution also. Sudden systems change is rarely very satisfactory. Change tends to be accepted best when the climate of opinion is ready for it; change opens the door to unknown sets of problems; so it is prudent to evolve towards the goal — and not to rush towards it.

Over the next few years we can expect to see greater progress in the area of computer networks. We can expect far better COBOL compilers on minicomputers and the language extended to handle on-line working more naturally. No doubt the mainframe manufacturers will wish to capitalise on the trend by providing migration paths from their larger machines to their smaller machines (quite a reversal over the last ten years). All of these trends will help the evolution towards distributed computing.

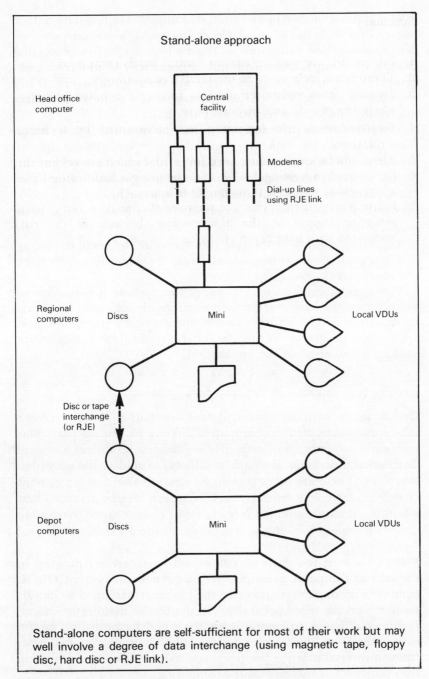

Stand-alone computers are self-sufficient for most of their work but may well involve a degree of data interchange (using magnetic tape, floppy disc, hard disc or RJE link).

Figure 1.11   Stand-alone computers in a hierarchical organisation structure

Summary

1. Cost trends are moving against central batch computers.
2. There is a strong move to interactive computing.
3. Pressure from computer users is forcing computer power to where the people and problems are.
4. Business needs are becoming less constrained by technical limitations.
5. There will be a continuing need for central systems development.
6. Distributed processing can be achieved using a mainframe-based approach as well as a minicomputer approach.
7. Existing investments constrain the pace of change — but gradual evolution should be the aim anyway, because of the risks associated with over-rapid change.

2 Identifying the business need and organisational impact of distributed systems

The steady move to on-line systems and distributed processing puts greater pressure on business analysts to understand the business applications. Mistakes are no longer buffered by the data control function — they are all too visible. The purpose of this chapter is to examine ways of gaining real business understanding (both operating needs and management control information) and to look at the impact of the VDU on that business need.

Looking back on the developments in computing over the last twenty years it is difficult to find any significant commercial computer application which was right first time. All too often three or more attempts are necessary — perhaps along the following lines. The DP department with an imperfect and simplistic understanding of the problem gets something working quite quickly (remarkably quickly in retrospect). Typically the solution is weak in two respects: it does not satisfy all the business needs and it lacks many of the rigorous control disciplines necessary in computer systems. But the system is working.

It is clearly necessary to profit from the lessons of this mistake. We will try again but this time the users resolve that they will be in the driving seat. Typically this second solution is found to be weak in two different respects: it is over-complex in trying to satisfy every need and requirements are evolving (changing) up to the last minute. The system is likely to fail in integration testing.

At the third attempt the problem area is viewed in a more realistic way. The earlier experiences lead to recognition that good solutions demand discipline on the part of the user — there is a distinction between 'wants' and 'needs'. Greater understanding of the business need by the technicians reduces the number of exceptions — by making them part of the general case. Better understood requirements leads to a practical 'freezing' of the file design and record layouts, leading to better project management.

This example, while over-simplified, illustrates some of the problems of achieving success. A successful project requires a frozen set of requirements. Requirements can only be frozen when the application area is genuinely and fully understood. Freezing them any earlier is not the answer.

Understanding operating needs

In an attempt to gain this understanding and to avoid previous mistakes, elaborate surveys are often carried out in the expectation that analysts will understand the application better. These surveys are time-consuming and yet experience suggests that they are no guarantee of success.

The good systems analyst with previous experience in the area is likely to get it right — with even a short survey. The good analyst without experience in the area will usually not get it right — no matter how long the survey. Partly the problem exists because in our desire to effect improvements we are too keen to see the short-comings in the existing system. It is all too common for the analyst to identify three uses for a particular document, for example, only to discover later that there is a fourth use which he was not told about. On the whole it is safer to assume that all documents, audit trails and controls exist because they have been found necessary in the working of the system. It is easier to remove 'extras' when the new system is introduced than it is to replace missing elements. Such an assumption — all aspects of the existing system must be retained in some form in the new system — has an additional advantage. It will be that much easier to introduce the new system if the reports are familiar and it is seen to meet all existing requirements. It is also less risky.

Gaining experience

Given that a good analyst is not going to get an unfamiliar area right first time, how should we tackle an unfamiliar area? We could:

— buy a package solution;
— buy experience;
— face the problem of growing experience.

Accepting what exists

Gaining experience

What must be right

Reducing risks

Adapting to changing user requirements

Figure 2.1   Steps in understanding operating needs

There is general recognition that while a package may not be the total answer it can be perfectly acceptable in all but the most critical areas of the business — it will probably work at least as well as a first-attempt in-house solution anyway. A further advantage of the package approach is that it can be implemented in a reduced time-scale and can be used to gain computer experience for a later bespoke solution. Where a package is inappropriate (critical business area or nothing suitable exists) it is almost certainly worth buying experience from the outside. The critical areas are at the start of the project (the survey, evaluation and systems design stages). At the very least the expert must be called in to carry out a design review or it may be better for him to be recruited to the permanent staff. What you cannot afford to do is to start teaching some tyro what a despatch note looks like if you want a first-rate order-processing system that will last.

If there is no package that fits and no proven expertise available, then we shall have to do it the hard way — learn from experience. Given that the first attempt is not likely to be successful, logically we should aim to solve a reasonable part of the problem quickly. Users can understand and forgive mistakes of comprehension if the product is available quickly. It is much less easy for them to accept a two-year gestation period with it still not right.

What must be right

If we are to achieve any degree of operational success, there are three aspects of the design to get right:

1. day-to-day operation of the system;

2. file strategy;
3. file contents;

We are most likely to get the day-to-day operation of the system right if we ensure that if follows existing practices (as discussed earlier). The file strategy needs to be right for both the daily operational requirements and the management information needs (to be discussed below). The file contents need to be right in two senses: allowance has been made for every field that may be required and sufficient space has been allowed in every field to cater for growth and change. If the file contents and file strategy are right at the start, then the base exists to satisfy the business needs and to cope with considerable business evolution. Get the files wrong and a complete re-write is inevitable, sooner or later.

Reducing risks

We have seen that one way of reducing the risk of failure is to build on previous application experience. Of equal importance is the need to avoid complexity. The more complex the area, the more difficult it is to get it right. The more 'integrated' the solution, the less the chance of success — and conversely, the more stand-alone the solution the better the chance of success.

It is not surprising that users are looking for small stand-alone computers (perhaps for a single or limited set of applications). Generally they see that the implementation time-scale will be reduced and the risk of failure through interference also reduced. The emotive words are 'simple', 'quickly implemented', 'low risk' and 'stand alone'.

Integration of applications was a popular concept in the late 1960s. In practice it has often meant large inflexible groups of systems which are so interlocked that they are unresponsive to change. A looser coupling of application systems makes it easier for them to change individually without upsetting the balance of the whole. Implicit in this argument is the recognition that there is unlikely to be a single blanket solution which satisfies all applications within an organisation. To seek a single computer policy means forcing all problems to fit the chosen solution, however unsuitable. Computer costs are now low enough across the spectrum of available power to allow designers to consider the needs of the application first. It will remain prudent to set policy guidelines, however, so that there is no random proliferation of equipment — or at least to ensure that there is a standard method of information interchange.

Adapting to changing user requirements

There are perhaps three reasons why user requirements change:

1. Greater understanding of the system allows some aspects to be discontinued. Perhaps tight controls were introduced many years ago at an earlier system change and they are no longer appropriate. For example, there is little point in checking records twice because they are printed in two different sequences. Assuming controls have been built in, the computer will never unknowingly lose a record.
2. Greater understanding of the system reveals new and unexpected benefits. As confidence in the accuracy of the system grows, its output is likely to be used more and more. New reports are requested and existing reports are demanded with greater frequency.
3. 'Business creep' may mean that the original specification no longer satisfies the business need.

While these shifts in requirements are perhaps inevitable there are ways of minimising their impact. The first essential is to *be sure that the request is valid*. The implementation of any system is a difficult time, even when things go well. Problems which loomed large at the time can be seen as relatively minor in retrospect. Before making changes therefore the analyst should check the facts:

— is this likely to be a recurring problem or is it a bedding in problem?
— is the problem based on a business need or is it created by a constraint in this or another system?
— is the size of the problem being distorted or exaggerated?
— is the change likely to have repercussions within this or another system?

The second way of minimising problems is found in the design approach. Generally, accounting systems are stable; it is reporting which is subject to change. It follows that *report extraction should not be embedded in the update programs*. Provided that the file contents and strategy are correct, this division means that changes in the reporting requirements can be coped with comfortably. Of course if the data on the files is incomplete it is difficult to respond to new requirements. Happily, on-line systems tend to force the separation of the update and reporting, and they have another benefit too. It is more difficult to go live with errors so, although system testing takes rather longer than with batch systems, *there tend to be fewer errors in the operation of on-line systems.*

Understanding management information requirements

Having understood the operating needs we can turn to determining the management information requirements.

At one time it was thought that computer-based information systems would solve all the management information needs for a business. Considerable sums of money were spent pursuing this goal until it became clear that it was unattainable. Robert N. Anthony, in *Planning and Control Systems, A Framework for Analysis,* advanced the concept that information was for 'decision-making'; he further suggested classifying decisions into three broad groups:

— strategic planning;
— management control (tactical planning);
— operation control.

Strategic planning is concerned with deciding on the objectives of the organisation and the disposition of its major resources. Tactical planning is concerned with deciding how to use the resources (e.g. setting inventory control guidelines) to achieve these objectives. Operational control is the process of ensuring that specific jobs get done and targets are met (e.g. achieving the inventory guidelines). There is, of course, a continuum of decisions across the spectrum from strategic to operational and Figure 2.2 shows the information characteristics at the extremes.

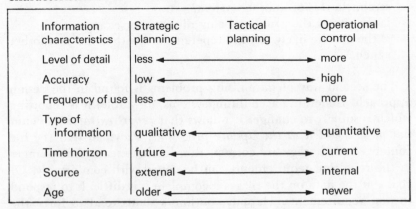

Information characteristics	Strategic planning	Tactical planning	Operational control
Level of detail	less ⟵		⟶ more
Accuracy	low ⟵		⟶ high
Frequency of use	less ⟵		⟶ more
Type of information	qualitative ⟵		⟶ quantitative
Time horizon	future ⟵		⟶ current
Source	external ⟵		⟶ internal
Age	older ⟵		⟶ newer

Figure 2.2 Analysis of information characteristics by class of decision

It can be seen that computer-based information is more likely to be helpful for operational control decisions where information needs are more detailed, more accurate, used frequently, internally derived etc. It is less likely to be helpful for strategic decisions where the information is qualitative, externally derived, concerned more with the future etc.

If management information is to be thought of as an hierarchy (as in figure 2.3) the shaded triangle represents the class of information that can never come as a by-product of the operational systems (such things as external pressures and innovation).

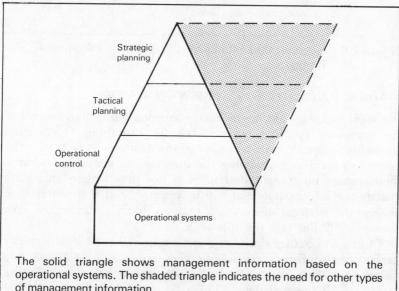

The solid triangle shows management information based on the operational systems. The shaded triangle indicates the need for other types of management information.

Figure 2.3   Management information hierarchy

It follows that the systems analyst, when designing a new operational system, should not spend too much time worrying about the tactical and strategic decisions. He must, however, consider management information needs at the operational control level.

That is not to say that the computer is always unhelpful at these higher levels of abstraction. Michael S. Scott Morton at MIT has shown that there is a second dimension to decision making, that of structured, semi-structured and unstructured decisions. While it is true that most operational decisions are or can be structured, and many strategic decisions are unstructured, there are many decisions at all three levels which are semi-structured. It is in this area that *decision support systems* are likely to be developed — using computers to gain greater understanding of the problem but always allowing the manager to override the computer model on the occasions when judgement is superior to straight logic. Generally, however, decision support systems are outside the scope of the systems analyst looking at operational systems.

Operational control of the business

Analysing information needs by class of decision

Deciding the data content of master files

Structuring transaction files

Figure 2.4   Steps in understanding management information
requests

Analysing information needs by classes of decision

We must be clear that operational control is more than control of the computer system (control totals for example). Operational control is designed to *assist control of the business.* How then is the analyst to set about analysing the information needs and what is their impact on systems design? It is not practical to anticipate exactly the information that will be required but it *is* practical to analyse the *patterns of decisions* that are likely to be needed. An example will illustrate the approach.

A foreign exchange dealing system is required to process currency deals, print confirmations to customers, send payment and receive instructions, keep track of overseas account balances and keep a record of all forward deals. These requirements are part of the operational system. Looking for the operational control requirements, the analyst is quickly going to establish the need for:

— control on limits and exposure by customer;
— outstanding deals by customer reports;
— profitability by type of deal and currency;
— position in a currency on some future date.

What we need to look for however is some consistent pattern in these requirements. In this case the analyst (who was experienced and had a very good understanding of the business) established that all queries were likely to fall into two patterns:

— what are the deals outstanding for a given customer?
— what is the position in a given currency on a particular day?

His hypothesis was tested against all practical types of query that could be devised and satisfied all requirements. The file design that resulted was organised to satisfy both patterns of question efficiently as well as the routine operational system.

This example shows the need for the file structures and access methods to be right as well as the file contents. More generally, it is on transaction records where we need to be most concerned about structure and access methods, while on master records content is the chief concern. The reason is that most master records have a dominant key while most transaction records have more than one.

Deciding the data content of master files

Take, for example, a customer master file. There is always the need for random access to a particular customer as well as sequential access. Perhaps the need for random access is more obvious than that of sequential access but they are equally necessary. Reports must show customers' details in a consistent way; similar names need to be displayed together as well as the branches for a particular customer. The customer file therefore has a natural sequence — similarly the product file, personnel file and supplier file. The problem is to ensure that all reasonable analysis codes and all the data fields required are built in. An analyst without previous experience of order-processing and stock control has virtually no chance of getting the contents of, say, a product master file right. Test your ability to do so before looking at the checklist in Figure 2.5. The lesson is clear. Build on other people's experience rather than try to get it right from scratch.

Structuring transaction files

Transaction records pose something of a data content problem (is it enough to hold the customer code or should full name and address details be held with the transaction? What analysis codes may be needed by class of transaction?) but mainly the problem is one of access. Should the open order file be held by customer number, product number or order number? A case can be made for all three; certainly access will be required by all three. The final sequence will be a balance between practical efficiency (which favours the order number approach) and patterns of queries (which probably favours the customer number approach). A good solution for most situations would be to insert orders sequentially as they are received and hold a list of orders by customer. The product position is held in summary on the product file.

This concept of analysing operational control information needs by patterns of decisions and queries leads to a better understanding of information needs. It also leads to a more practical technical design, which is not dominated by one-off or unrepresentative needs.

Organisational implications

The steady move to on-line data entry has come about now that it is technically risk-free and low cost. Batch data entry has always been slow, cumbersome and expensive, primarily because of the 'middlemen' required. VDUs allow the power of the computer to be located in the work place where the application knowledge resides. Nevertheless there are a number of traps to be avoided if the on-line system is to work at its full potential.

VDU input is different from batch input

The first problem is a legacy of 'batch' computer thinking. It is very common to discover analysts designing VDU screens to look like the forms the clerk is accustomed to using. A very sound approach — provided that the form does not exist only because of an earlier batch system. It is as easy to transcribe on to a VDU screen as it is to transcribe on to an intermediate document. So the analyst might be right, but he should be looking behind the existing forms to the source of the data.

Another example of 'batch thinking' is the need for codes. Unique codes are an integral part of any system, but when computers were first introduced the codes tended to be both visible and all numeric. With on-line systems the codes need not be numeric, nor need they be visible. The SWIFT (Society for the World-wide Interchange of Financial Transactions) message switch, for example, is used by banks to send money transfer instructions internationally. Messages are entered using VDUs and every field has a code, some of which are quite complex. Field '32A', for example, means Amount and Value Date. But on some message types the field code is '32B' and on others it is '33'. Some analysts got over the problem by inserting '32A/32B/33' against the field on the form. The operator would insert the amount and value whenever the VDU prompt said '32A' or '32B' or '33'. But the fact that SWIFT uses these codes need be of no concern to the operator. The VDU prompt also displays AMOUNT and VALUE DATE? So why not write these field names on the input form and dispense with the codes?

Header record
Stock item number
Warehouse number (00)
Record type (30)
Product group
Description
Unit of measure
Weight (Kg)
Volume (l)
Catalogue page/line no
Substitute number
Inventory valuation classification
Sales analysis code
Flags
Stock count cycle (days)
Date of next stock count

Stock movements information
Warehouse number
Bin/location no.

Current period
Beginning inventory
Transfers and adjustments
Receipts
Returns
Issues
Demand

Inventory on hand
Physical
Allocated
Outstanding
Forward
On order balance

Today's transactions
Receipts
Returns
Issues
Transfers in
Transfers out
Adjustments +
Adjustments −
Substitutions
Scrap
Stocktake
On order
Cancellations
Stock allocation

Buyer data
Warehouse no.
Order point
Safety stock
Minimum order qty
Maximum order qty
Multiple
Buyer's code

Primary source
Supplier account no.
Short name
Lead time
Re-order unit of measure
Supplier's product no.

Secondary source
Third source

Buying history
Warehouse no.

Last order details
Order date
Supplier no.
Order no.
Order status
Delivery date
Quantity ordered
Quantity received
Price per

Penultimate order details
Ante-penultimate order details

Price and financial data
Warehouse no.
Minimum order quantity
Recommended retail price
List price — Scale 1
List price — Scale 2
List price — Scale 3
List price — Scale 4
Special price
Start date
End date
Discount %/price indicator
Quantity break 1
Discount/price 1
Quantity break 2
Discount/price 2
Quantity break 3
Discount/price 3
Quantity break 4
Discount/price 4
Quantity break 5
Discount/price 5

Standard cost price
Valuation price (wtd avge)
Valuation price (realisable val)
Net sales value this period
Net sales value Y.T.D.
Cost of purchases this period
Cost of purchases Y.T.D.
Units purchased Y.T.D.

Usage history
Warehouse no.
Demand — 13 periods running
  most recent first $4P \times 13$
Net issues — 13 periods running
  most recent first $4P \times 13$

Control record
Stock item number (all Zs)
Warehouse no. (00)
No. of stock lines on file
No. of records on file

(Source: MBM Computers Ltd)

Figure 2.5   **Product master file checklist**

If codes do need to be used, let us at least try to make them meaningful. M, S, W, D for Married, Single, Widowed, Divorced is so much easier to remember than 1, 2, 3, 4; M&S for Marks and Spencer is quicker and more reliable than 8312575. Product codes present a more difficult problem, unless we can get the customer to order using the correct code. The analyst should always try to avoid code look-up and coding errors.

These examples illustrate the way VDU input differs from the batch type input procedures that have grown up. **Avoid putting the batch solution on-line: it is the business problem we are trying to put on-line.**

Siting the VDUs

The second potential trap is deciding where to site the VDUs. On a batch input payroll system it is common to find the payroll section in the accounts department because of the figure work involved and the need for accounting accuracy. But it is the personnel department which initiates all salary changes so should they not have a terminal of their own for entering changes and examining the file?

When deciding where to site VDUs the guiding rule is that **where one section is responsible for the control of a file** (for making sure it is up to date and that all changes are carried out correctly) **then that section only should carry out the input.** There are fewer links in the chain, so costs are reduced, and if anything does go wrong no time will be lost on an inter-section 'not my fault' squabble.

The rule looks clear enough but it is sometimes less easy to apply in practice. Some managers find it more comfortable to have another section to blame when things go wrong. They are unlikely to welcome a system where their failings are more exposed.

Putting the VDUs where responsibility for the file lies usually means the input is done in the originating department. The sales ledger is input from the accounts office, purchase ledger from the purchasing department and order-processing in the sales office. The exception comes when several departments use the same master file. It is not good practice to have different departments making changes to a master file. It is too easy to lose control. One section should be given the responsibility for the file and (applying the rule) only they should make the mainfile amendments. Other sections may have access to the files but may not amend them.

Siting the VDUs within the department

Once an application area has been identified and it is resolved to install VDUs within a department, there still remains a problem of how to organise them best. Should VDUs be operated by specialist staff or as a by-product of the clerical activity? A case study based on the experience of an investment management company illustrates the opportunities. The company manages portfolios on behalf of pension funds and private clients. Computers are used to prepare contract notes (confirming a purchase or a sale) and to maintain the client's portfolios for record keeping, valuations, dividend payment, etc. The first computer systems were introduced in the late 1960s with punched card input. Punched cards proved to be unsatisfactory and a revised input system was introduced using TC500 computer terminals. The TC500 machines produced contract notes for clients and a by-product paper tape for the computer accounting system was run overnight.

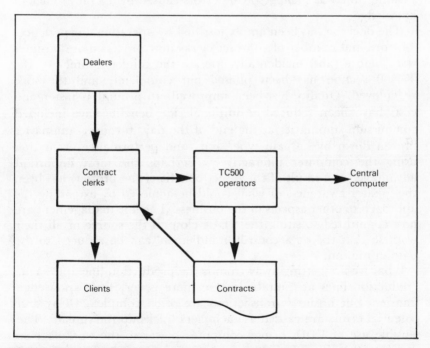

Figure 2.6   How should the VDUs be organised?

When considering how best to replace the TC500s with a minicomputer, four main ways of organising the VDU workflow were identified:

1. Replace the TC500 section with a VDU section (keep existing work flow, save one or two TC500 operators).
2. Have specialist VDU operators but attach them to the contract clerks (less paper movement, save an operator and a contract clerk).
3. Give VDUs to the contract clerks (cut out all the TC500 operators).
4. Merge the contract clerk's function with the dealers and give them all VDUs (the most radical change).

Solutions 1 and 4 were quickly ruled out; solution 1 because it offered no real benefits over the existing system, solution 4 because there were business reasons for separating the dealing function from the contracts back-up. The decision lay between solutions 2 and 3. For *this* business, solution 3 looked right. The business is highly technical and it was suspected that much of the contract clerks' existing time was spent resolving errors caused by operators' lack of knowledge.

The decision has been amply justified by operational experience. The original number of contract clerks now process more business than before (and incidentally operate the minicomputer) — the TC500 section has been phased out completely and the staff redeployed. Quality has been improved, turnround is faster and costs have been reduced. Additional side benefits have included commission summaries at the end of the day, turnover summaries broken down by bargain type, and fund performance evaluation using the computer interactively. Perhaps the most important advantage (as a result of the direct benefit of the project) has been the greater awareness of what could be achieved by extending the approach to other aspects of the business. The line management are now committed to siting the VDUs close to the source of all their work so that the data control 'middlemen' can be reduced to the bare minimum.

What we are getting away from is the production line approach. Production lines are suitable where there is very little knowledge transfer. But business transactions are often complex. Delay and potential errors are caused as each clerk 'picks up the thread'. The sensible use of VDUs brings computer power to the workplace so that (ideally) all operations can be carried out with a minimum of paper movement.

Impact of on-line systems on business organisation

Figure 2.7 illustrates the way the introduction of computers has

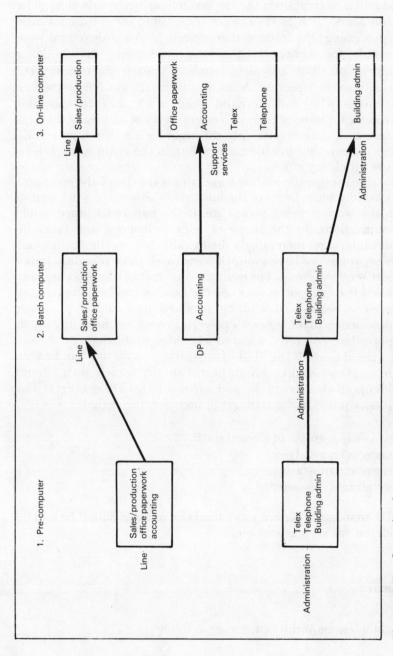

Figure 2.7   Organisation structure evolving with the use of computers

affected the structure of some organisations. Before the introduction of computers the responsibilities were fairly clear. The line functions, such as sales, were responsible for getting business and processing the orders that resulted. Administration were responsible for services such as telex, telephone and building administration. The arrival of batch computers inserted the DP function into the structure. Most of the impact was felt by the line departments who had to hand their work over to this new department for some of their processing. It is not surprising that this structure took time to settle into the organisation; batch processing is often clumsy, and inserting a new link in the chain is unlikely to improve efficiency much.

The third stage, the on-line stage, shows the use of the computer extended into more facets of the business. VDUs at the work station mean the work is being picked up at the paperwork stage, while communications, in the shape of telex, telephone and facsimile transmission, are increasingly being affected by the computer. Many organisations have grouped some or all these functions into a 'support services' group. For example, one manufacturing company has based their support services on the existing production planning department. Sales go out and sell, production produce to plan, but it is production planning (with powerful computer back-up) which accepts orders, controls stocks and schedules production.

The trend towards this kind of organisation structure can be seen also in insurance, banking and the distributive trades. Such a trend provides both an opportunity and a threat to the DP manager. The qualities required in the manager of such a service include:

— man-management of clerical staff;
— business knowledge;
— computer knowledge;
— accountancy knowledge.

The DP manager will need more than one of these skills if he is to be considered for such a position.

Summary

The main lessons of this chapter are as follows:

1. Make a determined effort to introduce new systems more effectively by building on previous experience.

2. Ensure all aspects of the existing day-to-day operation are covered by the new system. Consider especially the need for operational control information.
3. Avoid putting a batch computer solution on to an on-line system. Get back to the business need.
4. Recognise that siting VDUs in the work place will change the way it is managed and may have far-reaching organisational consequences.

3 Deciding the file strategy

The availability of inexpensive processors means that the systems designer does not have to worry about where to carry out processing — it can be done at reasonable cost in virtually any location in the business. The location of data files, however, presents a more difficult problem. At one extreme airline seat reservation systems must have a single central file; at the other extreme large independent divisions of an organisation will have their own files and systems. But what are the general guidelines?

The purpose of this chapter is to provide guidelines for developing a file strategy. We are not concerned with file organisation (that will be discussed in Chapter 5); we are concerned with the file location strategy. Before going into the design guidelines there are two principles to be established. First, there is unlikely to be a single solution for an organisation. The *ideal solution* will depend on the application and the *practical solution* will probably be a compromise between many applications. The point is that the **analysis should start on an application-by-application basis.** Secondly, all solutions will fall into one of the following three classes:

1. The files are centralised;
2. The files are local;
3. The files are part centralised and part local.

What we have ruled out in these solutions is the hierarchical organisation illustrated in Figure 3.1. The hierarchical organisation is a practical *equipment organisation* but it usually satisfies several applications. To some applications the depot files are local and the regional files central. To other applications the regional files are

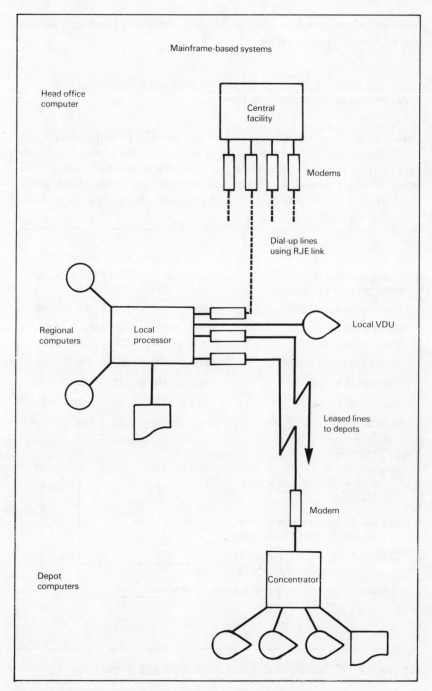

Figure 3.1 Hierarchical computer organisation

local and the depot files central. Having regional files merely affects the degree of centralisation.

Constraints of information flow

Now it is theoretically possible to solve all applications by centralising the files. In practice it is not always cost-effective or practical. The main reason is the limitation of information flow using data transmission. Figure 3.2, for example, provides a guide to what can be transmitted in an hour over various speeds of line.

	Leased lines			Dial-up lines	
Line speed (baud)	9600	4800	2400	1200	300
Assumed ch. rate (cps)	800	400	200	100	25
Total characters (000)	2880	1440	720	360	90
No. of 80 ch. records	36000	18000	9000	4500	1125
No. of 100 ch. records	28800	14400	7200	3600	900
Invoices of 5 lines (output)	3600	1800	900	450	112
Statements (output)	2880	1440	720	360	90
Report pages (output)	640	320	160	80	20
Invoices (input) with local screen formatting and editing	24000	12000	6000	3000	750
Invoices (input) with central screen formatting and editing	600	300	150	75	18

4800 baud: maximum assumed speed on leased lines

1200 baud: maximum synchronous transmission on dial-up lines

300 baud: maximum asynchronous transmission on dial-up lines

Figure 3.2   Guide to what can be transmitted in one hour

For calculation purposes it is wise to assume maximum transmission speeds of:

— 4800 baud on leased lines;
— 1200 baud synchronous on dial-up lines;
— 300 baud asynchronous on dial-up lines;

It can be seen from the figure that even at 1200 baud, quite substantial transmissions are possible — 450 five-line invoices in an hour *or* 360 customer statements *or* 80 pages of analysis reports. What can also be seen is the dramatic difference in invoice input speed when editing and screen formatting are carried out centrally rather than locally. This difference requires explanation.

Before data can be entered on the VDU, the screen format has to be displayed — perhaps 1500 characters (including protected fields) for the first screen (customer details). The order header information is entered — perhaps 40 characters which are then transmitted. The input is validated, customer name and address added, and it is redisplayed — perhaps another 1500 characters. Following acceptance, the next screen is displayed for invoice lines — and so on. It is not difficult to see that 6000 or so characters have to be transmitted although the raw input is only 120 to 150 characters. A reasonable rate of working for an operator would be one invoice entered per minute — which does not allow many terminals to a single line even at 4800 baud. In short, this approach is impractical if there is any significant volume of work. Even centralised systems, therefore, tend to have local intelligent terminals which hold screen formats, print formats and carry out basic input validation. They may also have skeleton product and customer files to permit more complete validation. Figure 3.3 illustrates the approach.

As a general rule all input should be validated in context. Experience shows that error correction is very error prone — for example, if a £100 credit entry has been posted incorrectly as a debit, the 'correcting' entry might easily be entered as:

— a £100 credit adjustment;
— a £200 credit adjustment; or
— a £100 debit adjustment.

The correct action is not obvious, particularly if the clerk is under time pressure. It is far more satisfactory not to make errors in the first place — by rigorously validating the input. Generally this input has to be validated against main files (or main file extracts) to

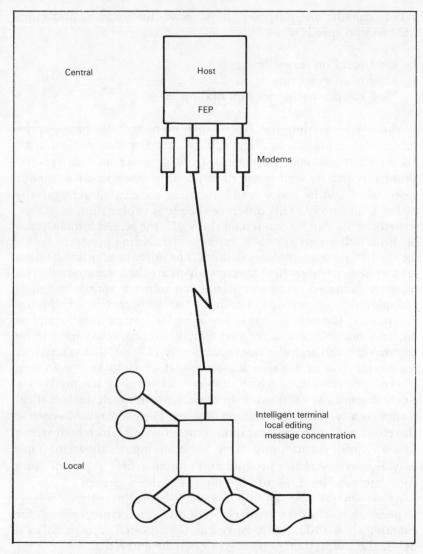

Figure 3.3   Using intelligent terminals to minimise input
data traffic

ensure, for example, that the product and the customer exist. There
are some situations where vetting can be done without main files —
for example cash input where the account number has a built-in check
digit and the amounts can be checked against add-listed totals.

So some degree of local intelligence is necessary to carry out this
validation function at remote sites. It is therefore not a big step (in
cost terms) to make this local processor more powerful or even free-

standing. To a first order therefore the cost of a distributed system from one manufacturer will be close to the cost of a centralised system from the same manufacturer. There is likely to be more difference in cost between manufacturers than between their solutions.

Arguments in favour of distributed files

We have seen why costs do not necessarily favour centralised files and that data vetting is improved with local files. Other arguments in favour of distributed files can be summarised as:

— more robust in case of failure (Figure 3.4 illustrates the point);
— local commitment to local ownership;
— reduced complexity from dividing up the problem;
— less risk of unauthorised access — no single access point;
— greater overall throughput by parallel working — avoiding file access bottlenecks.

It is also possible to increase complexity by distributing files. A full copy of the database at every site is dauntingly difficult to maintain. Segmenting the database with directories held locally also creates challenging problems of file management. Centralised files are better understood and are easier to manage than complex data networks. Other arguments in favour of centralised files can be summarised as:

— greater degree of control and discipline likely;
— reduced need for skilled operators locally;
— only practical way of controlling a shared resource (airline seats, theatre tickets, central stock items).

Given this background we can now move on to guidelines for deciding the overall file strategy.

Guidelines for deciding the file strategy

The starting point for deciding the way data files should be located is a good understanding of the business needs of this application. The author's book *A Guide to the Successful Management of Computer Projects* describes in Chapter 5 how to carry out a

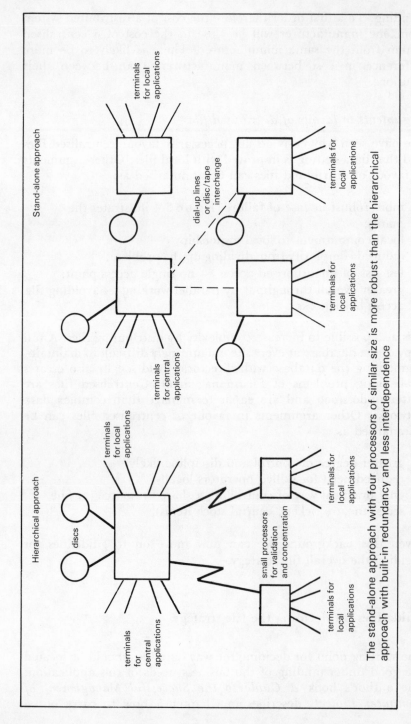

Figure 3.4 Hierarchical approach v stand-alone approach

business survey and how to identify the business *purpose* behind every activity.

Once real understanding of the business need has been accomplished, we can examine the following decision criteria:

1. File ownership;
2. Speed of response;
3. Volume of transactions;
4. Interaction with other systems.

File ownership

Distributed processing in our definition means locating terminals at the work place. Wider access to the computer and its files, however, must be accompanied by very clear understanding of who is responsible for the data when things go wrong. Split responsibility does not work, so the first issue is to decide where responsibility lies.

---

1. Personnel — payroll

2. Customers — sales ledger transactions

3. Suppliers — purchase ledger transactions

4. Financial — nominal ledger transactions
　　　　　　(including job and production costs)

5. Fixed assets register

6. Share register

7. Standard times and bills of material

8. Inventory of:　finished goods
　　　　　　　　parts
　　　　　　　　raw materials
　　　　　　　　supplies

9. Outstanding orders:　customers' back orders
　　　　　　　　　　　production orders
　　　　　　　　　　　purchase orders

10. Historical data and statistics

Figure 3.5 Checklist of main files

Figure 3.5 provides a checklist of master files and transactions for a typical organisation. As part of the business need (not computer need) it should be possible to determine rationally who should be responsible for a given file — or part of a file.

In an organisation with decentralised invoicing and centralised accounts it may be decided that every branch should be responsible for its own customers (customer master file) but responsibility for cash collection (sales ledger transactions) should be in the central accounts department. Or maybe it is decided to decentralise both invoicing and cash collection so the responsiblity for both customer and sales ledger transactions files should be with the branch. Inevitably there is an interaction between what happens (invoicing) and the file ownership (customer file) and it is helpful if the system designer challenges both assumptions. Is invoicing decentralised because customer details are held locally? Or are customer details held locally because invoicing is decentralised? What would be the impact of centralised invoicing with central responsibility for customers? The general rule is that **a file should be held as close as possible to the section responsible for its accuracy.**

Speed of response

It is quite common to have many users of a file even though there should be only one owner. The warehouse manager is the one responsible for physical stock but the stock level will be of value to several parts of the organisation. Different users have differing needs in terms of response time. For example, staff allocating stock need a quick response while central accounts (who need month-end figures) can wait a day or so. Requests from remote depots can usually be delayed a little — after all it will take a considerable time physically to move the stock item from one depot to the other so a few minutes' delay for the enquiry can be tolerated. The general rule is that **files should be held as close as possible to the section requiring the fastest response.**

Volume of transactions

Frequency of use and volume of transactions tend to be synonymous in many systems. We need to establish where the greatest volume of transactions originates and who are the most frequent users of the files. The general rule is that **files should be held close to where the largest volumes of transactions originate** or where there is the greatest frequency of use.

Interaction with other systems

Few systems exist in isolation. There is often a degree of interaction with other systems, one of which may have dominating requirements. For example, central clearing of cheques tends to mean that banks hold all accounts centrally. It is true that in this example centralisation makes it easier to enquire about a given account from any branch, but enquiries are rarely the dominant reason for locating files; operational requirements are more significant. The general rule is to **establish clearly the constraints imposed by other systems.** A problem to be recognised is that some constraints are artificial — they are not external constraints but are the product of a previous internal system. Self-imposed constraints of this nature should be ignored at this stage. First work out what is desirable before deciding what is practical (a point picked up in the next few pages).

Splitting files by time-scale

Most applications can be divided conveniently into two time-frames. Stock *recording*, for example, usually requires a quick response with real-time updating of the stock levels. Stock *control,* however, is impractical on a minute-by-minute basis. Realistically, stock control runs are carried out daily, twice a week or even weekly. It would thus be possible to carry out stock recording locally and stock control centrally. The product file, in this example, would need to be split. The master copy would be at the centre (complete with buyer information, purchase orders and order-chasing details), while subsets of the file would be held locally (descriptions, prices and stock levels). The general rule is to **recognise that files can be split but that the master copy needs to be identified clearly.**

	Files should be close	Files may be remote
	←――――――――――――――――――→	
Ownership:	Responsible for data accuracy	Enquiry only
Response time:	Fast response needed	Slow response adequate
Volume and frequency:	High volumes originate	Low volumes
Recognise:	External system constraints Splitting files by time-scale Organisational constraints	

Figure 3.6   File location guidelines

Deciding on file location

Figure 3.6 summarises the rules we have established for locating the files. For a given application, therefore, the system designer identifies the main files and establishes the ideal location. Not surprisingly, the various rules usually combine together to point to a single solution — because the file 'owners' tend to need the quickest response and tend to generate the highest volume of file activity. In cases where the rules conflict, the system designer will have to build a model of the various alternatives and evaluate them carefully. In particular he must take account of the constraints imposed by the organisation and its existing computer investment.

Organisational constraints

We shall look at organisational constraints under the following headings:

— existing computer investment;
— business culture;
— local economies of scale;
— reducing risk.

None of these headings will dominate the final solution but they are all likely to influence it and to determine the pace of change.

Existing computer investment

It is undesirable to make changes to systems which are working well (without good reason). Even if change is desirable it is preferable to move one step at a time, making sure that each step is secure before going on to the next. Look, therefore, for ways of retaining the good elements of existing systems. In particular, if an application runs in two time-cycles, change only one at a time. It is usually impractical to carry out shift working at every local site so consider running overnight and peak batch loads at the centre, capitalising on existing investment.

Business culture

The management style of the organisation will have been taken into account already — when considering who should 'own' the files.

Other aspects of the business culture to consider are:

— attitude to DP;
— attitude to central management services;
— staffing remote sites.

If the central management services are highly regarded they will be able to recommend either a central or a local solution with credibility. A central management service which has lost the confidence of the users will find increasing resistance to more centralisation. In fact, any strong pressure for local control should be viewed with sympathy as the local site will be more committed to its success.

On the other hand the staffing of remote sites with competent operators is not a trivial problem. The more the files are centrally controlled, the fewer the local skills that are necessary. Completely distributed files means the enforcement of local security and back-up procedures. The availability of suitable local staff will thus influence the decision also.

Local economies of scale

So far the designer should have been looking at his application in as much isolation as possible. There then comes the time to consider the overall hardware need. We have seen that it is unwise to expect a single blanket hardware solution to cover all applications; nevertheless we do need to look for a hardware solution which is acceptable in the organisation. A practical approach is to **look for local economies of scale.**

The hardware might be located physically:

— by geographic location;
— by business unit;
— by application/processing time-cycle.

Often geographic location and business unit are synonymous, but there are situations where different divisions are located at the same site. Should they each have their own computer hardware? Should they all share a common facility? Or should there be a bit of both?

Intuitively it looks less expensive to have a single facility and this solution will be the most practical in a stable business environment. The approach, however, is likely to restrict change should any division be growing, or indeed shrinking. If a common facility is needed, experience suggests that it should be run by the central management services people — not by one of the divisions on behalf of the others — there will be practical problems of priorities and working hours unless the needs of the divisions buying time are relatively small.

Organising the computer facility by business unit tends to be the most satisfactory approach. Responsibility for the business and the computer solution are the same, so priority conflicts can be resolved 'in-house' while achieving local economies of scale.

There are situations, also, when an application justifies its own hardware solution: at a simple level, the use of a time-sharing bureau for a particular application rather than an in-house facility; perhaps a large application which can justify separate hardware; a problem area which needs its own specialist solution; or a package solution working on dedicated hardware.

The point has already been made that many applications are run in two time-scales and the need exists to consider both time-scales separately. Shift working at remote sites is inefficient, expensive and difficult to manage so here is a fairly natural area for the centre.

Reducing risk

The over-riding requirement is that the chosen solution should work well in satisfying the business need. Resist the temptation, therefore, to attempt too much that is new. The unknown is rarely simpler than you imagine so plan to build progressively. A common hardware/software policy for the organisation ensures that the lessons learned in one area will be useful in other applications. Different hardware for every application creates the greatest degree of risk and is a false economy. If different hardware is necessary (as it probably is at some point in a computer hierarchy) looking for **program portability across levels is a further way of reducing risk.** The processing power can be geared to the size of the business unit with a minimum of disruption if there is growth or if the design turns out to have been over-optimistic.

Summary

1. Cost arguments do not particularly favour centralised files.
2. Each application should be considered separately — there is not likely to be a single best solution for an organisation.
3. Ideally, files and processing should be close to the main user (owner) for a given application.

4. The ideal solution is constrained by the existing computer investment and the need for local economies of scale.
5. Whatever solution is selected, change should be evolutionary so that the risk of failure is minimised.

4 Communications networks

By the late 1960s mainframe computers were well advanced and batch computing was well understood. Large central computers matched the centralised style of management then in vogue, and they also offered processing economies of scale. However, the need remained to communicate with remote locations — a need satisfied by 'remote job entry' (RJE) terminals. The IBM 2780 RJE terminal became the industry standard for connecting remote card readers and printers to central mainframes. The 2780 method of working has subsequently been improved to include data compression (for example, repeated space characters on a report do not have to be sent individually) and more interactive working. It has also become a practical standard for communicating between minicomputers and mainframes or between different manufacturers' machines.

We therefore start this chapter on communications networks by looking at the 2780 protocol in more detail (as an example of point-to-point communication between computers). We then go on to look at different ways of connecting VDUs to minicomputers and mainframes. The final section of the chapter looks at the development of computer networks and the transmission techniques they require.

2780 point-to-point communications

Remote job entry (RJE) is a method of operation that allows a batch job to be entered at a remote site, processed on a central computer and the results printed back at the remote site. Input was originally

Remote job entry (RJE)

Block

Block check character (BCC)

Longitudinal redundancy check (LRC)

Cyclic redundancy check (CRC)

Baud

Leased line

Line conditioning

Modem (modulator-demodulator)

Synchronous transmission

Binary synchronous communications (also BSC or Bisynch)

Protocol

Control character

Transparent mode

Character stuffing

Data compression

Figure 4.1   Concepts of 2780 point-to-point communications
explained in this section

by punched card and output went to a line printer (or card punch).

Because RJE links were originally used for card reading and printing it was sensible to use a method of operation that sent several cards or lines at a time — i.e. *blocks* of data. Furthermore, it was essential that there were no data transmission errors. With every block of data, therefore, is sent a *block check character*. This block check character is calculated by carrying out a *longitudinal redundancy check* or a *cyclic redundancy check*. The check character is accumulated at both the sending and the receiving stations during the transmission of a block. It is transmitted as the last character in the block and if it is the same as the check character calculated at the receiver, the block is accepted. Otherwise re-transmission is requested.

The RJE transmission method, therefore, was designed to send blocks of error-free data down a communications link — a major reason for its continued acceptance as a method of communicating between computers.

The physical connection between terminal and computer (or computer and computer) is made by telephone line. At low speeds (up to 2400 *baud* — i.e. 2400 bits per second) it is possible to use dial-up lines. At higher speeds — 4800 or 9600 baud — it is necessary to use *leased lines* which are usually *conditioned* by the PTT to ensure a high quality connection.

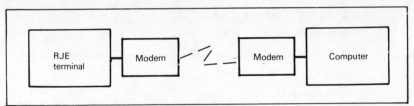

Figure 4.2   Modems are used to transmit streams of bits over voice grade lines

Even with line conditioning it is not possible to send digital signals down a telephone line (dial-up or leased) as a stream of pulses. They may cause false operation of trunk equipment or pick up unwanted signals. To overcome the problem, devices known as *modems* (modulator-demodulator) convert the stream of bits into an audible signal for reliable transmission. The modem works in both directions, demodulating incoming signals. Different modems are available for different speeds of transmission.

During the transmission the data bits are transmitted at a fixed rate (for example, 2400 baud as mentioned earlier) with the receiving modem synchronised with the transmitter. The receiver locks on to the carrier wave from the transmitter so it knows when to look for phase changes. This *synchronous transmission* is suitable for use at speeds up to 9600 baud or greater over suitably conditioned leased lines. On wideband circuits, speeds of around 50 kilobaud are achieved. The IBM 2780 uses synchronous transmission using a defined set of control characters to control the transmission — known as *binary synchronous communications*.

In fact the 2780 uses a defined *protocol* for establishing and maintaining the communication session. This protocol is analogous to a telephone conversation along the lines of Figure 4.3. 'ENQ', 'ACK' and 'NAK' are examples of *control characters* which are used to initiate, modify or stop communication sequences. 'ACK, 0' and 'ACK, 1' are used alternately to acknowledge successful receipt of transmission — providing a check that one of the blocks has not been totally lost. Using these control characters can present a problem — if we wish to send a data character which happens itself to be a control character. It is important that this data character gets through to the receiver intact and without upsetting the transmission — known as *transparent mode* transmission.

Telephone conversation		Computer protocol	
Sender	Receiver	Terminal	Computer
'I have a message for you'		'ENQ'	
	'Go ahead'		'ACK,O'
Sentence 1		Data Block 1	
	'OK'		'ACK,1'
Sentence 2		Data Block 2	
	'Please repeat'		'NAK'
Sentence 2		Data Block 2	
	'OK'		'ACK,O'
Sentence 3		Data Block 3	
	'OK'		'ACK,1'
'I have finished'		'EOT'	

Figure 4.3   Telephone conversation and computer protocol compared

In transparent binary synchronous communications, control characters are preceded by a data link escape (DLE) character. If it is desired to send a DLE character as part of the data, then a DLE character is inserted by the transmitter to indicate that the second DLE is data. This method of achieving data transmission transparency is known as *character stuffing*. Generally the transparent mode of transmission is not supported in 2780 implementations.

The 2780 protocol is not suitable for links with a long propagation delay (e.g. satellite links) as every block must be acknowledged. The effective transmission rate is halved and in extreme cases time-out will occur.

Asynchronous transmission

So far we have been looking at the transmission methods which were developed for remote job entry terminals. Quite a different method of transmission was developed for telegraph and telex circuits. On these circuits operators can key directly to a remote teleprinter character by character. Typing speeds of course vary considerably and an exactly even flow of characters cannot be guaranteed. There is thus the need to transmit on a character-by-character basis. This mode of transmission is known as *asynchronous transmission*.

Asynchronous transmission

ASCII

EIA interface (RS232C or V24)

Current loop (20mA)

Duplex (full duplex)

Half duplex

Acoustic coupler

Multiplexing

Frequency division multiplexing

Time division multiplexing

Front-end processor

Multipoint line

Polling

Contention

Concentrator

Figure 4.4   Concepts of using interactive VDUs explained in this section

With asynchronous transmission each character is enclosed with start and stop bits. For example, ASCII characters are sent typically as ten bits:

— start bit;
— seven data bits (ASCII code);
— parity bit;
— stop bit.

When the receiver detects the start bit it begins sampling the line at a predetermined rate (typically 110 baud or 300 baud for printing terminals; 1200, 2400 or 9600 baud for VDUs). The presence or absence of a signal at the expected time is translated into a '1' or a '0'. The time interval between the bits of a character is even but the interval between characters may be of unequal length. In practice, all current on-line computers can have asynchronous terminals connected using the standard ASCII character set shown in Figure 4.5.

The British Standard Data Code
(ISO 7-bit Code; ASCII; CCITT Alphabet No 5)

Column / Row	0	1	2	3	4	5	6	7
0	NUL	DLE	SP	0	@	P		p
1	SOH	DC1	!	1	A	Q	a	q
2	STX	DC2	''	2	B	R	b	r
3	ETX	DC3	£ or #	3	C	S	c	s
4	EOT	DC4	$	4	D	T	d	t
5	ENQ	NAK	%	5	E	U	e	u
6	ACK	SYN	&	6	F	V	f	v
7	BEL	ETB	'	7	G	W	g	w
8	FE0(BS)	CAN	(	8	H	X	h	x
9	FE1(HT)	EM	)	9	I	Y	i	y
A	FE2(LF)	SUB	*	:	J	Z	j	z
B	FE3(VT)	ESC	+	;	K	[	k	{
C	FE4(FF)	IS4(FS)	,	<	L	\	l	|
D	FE5(CR)	IS3(GS)	—	=	M	]	m	}
E	SO	IS2(RS)	.	>	N	^	n	— or ~
F	SI	IS1(US)	/	?	O	_	o	DEL

Each position in the code table is specified by its column and row
e.g. A is the position 41.

Figure 4.5 Standard ASCII character set

There are two standard terminal interfaces possible for asynchronous working — EIA and current loop. The *EIA interface* (also known as RS232C or V24) uses high and low voltage levels for the digital signalling and is the interface needed for connection to most modems (for remote working). The voltage level is measured relative to ground — which causes two problems. First, the sending and receiving stations need to be at the same ground potential;

second, the voltage level may be affected by other electromagnetic fields. As a consequence it is difficult to guarantee error-free working at high speed (9600 baud) at distances greater than a few hundred feet (EIA maximum is officially 50 feet). The *current loop interface* (also known as 20 or 60 milliamp) depends on the presence or absence of a current for the digital signalling and is more suitable for driving in-house VDUs up to 2000 feet distant. First, no ground plane is needed; secondly, any electromagnetic force affects both wires together. The voltage difference remains the same and the signal is less affected. The table 4.1 gives a guide to practical working distances:

Table 4.1

Speed	V24 (RS232C) (shielded cable)	Current loop (20mA) (twisted pair cable)
9600 baud	200 feet	500 feet
4800 baud	500 feet	1000 feet
2400 baud	1000 feet	2000 feet

When comparing transmission methods, asynchronous working has the following advantages:

1. Characters can be sent as they occur, because each character has its own synchronising information.
2. It is particularly suitable for keyboards, unbuffered terminals (e.g. paper tape reader) and real-time data collection.
3. It is an easy and inexpensive way of driving mechanical equipment (e.g. character printers).

The disadvantages are:

1. Speed is limited because separate timing is required in receiver and transmitter and a margin for error must be built in (5 per cent tolerance per bit can become 50 per cent after 10 bits)
2. Error checking is not usually built into the transmission (mechanical devices may not check parity either)
3. Transmission of data blocks is a little inefficient because of the start and stop bits added to every character

The synchronous method of transmission has the following advantages:

1. Very much higher speeds can be achieved because of the common timing source along with the data.
2. Transmission of data blocks is more efficient because there are no stop/start bits on every character. All bits are data except the synchronising pattern at the start and the check characters at the end of every block.
3. Data can be sent as bit streams rather than as characters.
4. Error checking is usually built into the transmission protocol.

Its disadvantages are:

1. Characters cannot be sent as they become available; they must be buffered and sent synchronously.
2. The buffers add to the cost of terminal equipment and the modems are also more expensive.
3. A single bit in error can cause the entire message block to be faulty.

Using interactive VDUs

Broadly there are two ways of connecting terminals to a computer and a number of subdivisions within them:

— an entry port per terminal:
  • direct link;
  • modem link;
  • multiplexer link;
— a single entry port for many terminals (multipoint or multidrop):
  • direct polling;
  • using concentrators;
  • using intelligent terminals.

Figure 4.6 illustrates three different ways of connecting a terminal to a port. The local terminals can be connected (using either EIA or current loop) to run at speeds up to 9600 baud.

Two of the remote terminals are connected via modems to the central computer. Asynchronous working over telephone lines in this way is relatively slow. One type of modem allows transmission speeds of up to 300 baud in both directions at the same time. Another type (which is also used for Prestel) can transmit at 1200 baud in one direction and 75 baud in the other (known as

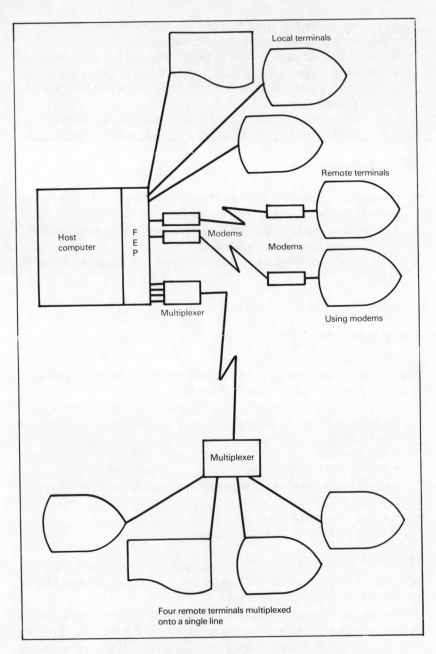

Figure 4.6   Ways of connecting terminals to a host computer with one entry port per terminal. A front end processor (FEP) is used to take the communication load off the host computer

asymmetrical duplex). The 75 baud rate is fast enough to accept keyboard typing speeds while the faster 1200 baud is used to display replies. Operation in both directions at the same time is known as *duplex* or *full duplex* working. Operation in one direction at a time is known as *half duplex*.

The table 4.2 shows the modems suitable for asynchronous and synchronous working for the British Post Office and Bell in the United States.

Table 4.2

Service	BPO Modem	Bell equivalent
300 baud full duplex asynch.	2	103A
300 baud full duplex asynch. (originate only)	13	113
1200 baud/75 baud asynch. or 1200 baud half duplex	1	202
1200 baud synch/2400 baud on leased lines	7 or 12	201A or 201B
4800/9600 baud synch.	private suppliers	

Using one modem per line is most suitable for dial-up lines where the terminals are geographically dispersed. Portable printing terminals are available complete with an *acoustic coupler*. The acoustic coupler is a modem which can be connected directly to a telephone handset — a tight push fit into a specially moulded receiver. Using such a printing terminal it is possible to dial up the computer from any location which has a telephone (as in Figure 4.7).

If several VDUs are geographically close together in a remote location it is wasteful to use a line for each one. Using a *multiplexer* it is possible for several low-speed terminals (up to 300 baud) to share a single leased line. The multiplexer acts as a number of modems, each one of which has a different frequency carrier wave so they can be combined on to a single line. This technique is known as *frequency division multiplexing*. A multiplexer is required at both ends of the line, as shown in Figure 4.6, so to the computer there appears to be one VDU per entry port.

Another technique is *time division multiplexing* in which bits (bit TDM) or characters (character TDM) are interleaved on a high-speed line. The local multiplexer de-multiplexes the bits or characters and presents them to the computer exactly as they

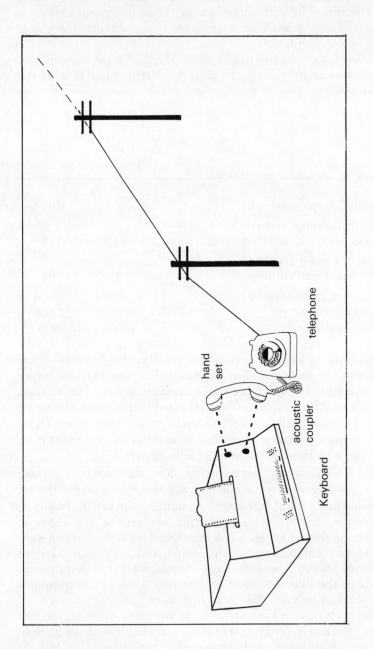

Figure 4.7 Using a portable terminal with built-in modem and acoustic coupler

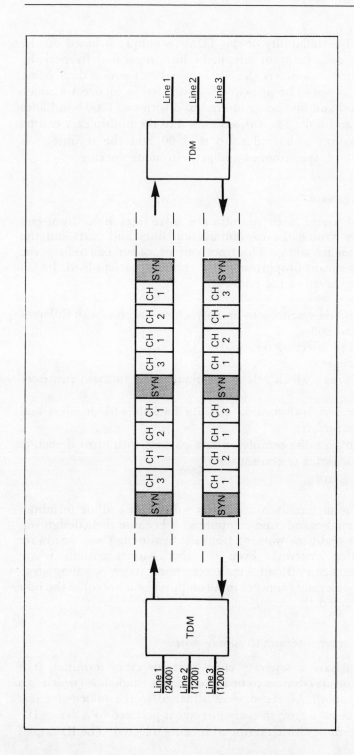

Figure 4.8 Transmission using time division multiplexing on a 4800 baud line

originated. The reliability of the TDM technique is based on the transmission of a constant stream of bits, separated by periodic synchronisation characters (SYN) — whether there is data being transmitted or not. The principle is illustrated in Figure 4.8 which shows a 2400 baud line being multiplexed with two 1200 baud lines on a 4800 baud link. The various lines into the multiplexer can be any combination which adds up to 4800 and the technique is suitable for both synchronous and asynchronous working.

Front-end processors

The current trend with mainframes is to attach a 'front-end processor' to handle the communication lines and carry out the basic protocol handling. The front-end processor can relieve the host of a significant proportion of the communications load. Its job involves some or all of the following:

— line control on synchronous and asynchronous ports with different speeds and codes;
— polling and selecting terminals;
— modem control;
— buffer storage which relates terminal speed to main processor speed;
— assembly and transmission of data packets with headers and check characters;
— reception and disassembly of data packets with error detection and requests for re-transmission;
— message routing.

In general, minicomputers are better suited to handling terminals than traditional mainframe computers — because their design was intended for real-time working from the beginning (both hardware and operating systems). Even so, there are situations where minicomputers can offload remote communications handling on to a front-end processor (another minicomputer or a micro) so the host is not overloaded.

Connecting several terminals to one port

Rather than have a separate entry port for every terminal, it is possible for several devices to be attached to a single line (which can be coaxial cable). All the devices attached to the *multipoint line* receive all the messages, so every message is prefixed by a device ID. The ID determines which terminal is being selected. The ID is used

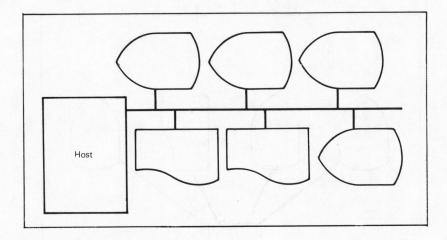

Figure 4.9   Multipoint line with polling

in a similar way when terminals are being *polled* to see if they have data ready to send in. The polling sequence is determined by the host computer and may be varied to give better service to some devices at the expense of others. A polling sequence of 'A-B-A-C-A-D' gives much better service to device 'A' than does the sequence 'A-B-C-D'. Terminals have to wait their turn to be polled but *contention* between them is avoided (two terminals sending messages at the same instant).

Concentrators are designed to make good use of lines to remote clusters of terminals. Instead of sending several messages slowly down the line at the same time (the multiplexer approach), concentration sends faster bursts one at a time. The concentrator acts as a buffer between the local terminals and the main processor and may change the transmission speed and internal code of the data being sent.

An example will illustrate the way concentrators use lines more efficiently than, say, TDM. Using TDM, two 2400 baud lines would be the maximum load for a 4800 baud link. But in reality the lines are idle for a significant proportion of the time. On a data entry application an operator would spend 60 seconds keying in 240 characters of data — transmitted in half a second at 4800 baud and perhaps one and a half seconds back (expanded). The line utilisation is only two seconds in every 60, i.e. $3\frac{1}{3}$ per cent. In practice there will be a mix of jobs, some of which have a higher transmission to data entry ratio, and the line must not be overloaded

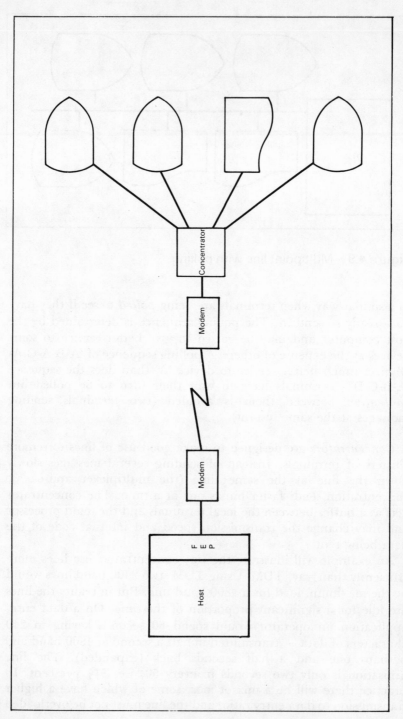

Figure 4.10   Using a remote concentrator to reduce line costs

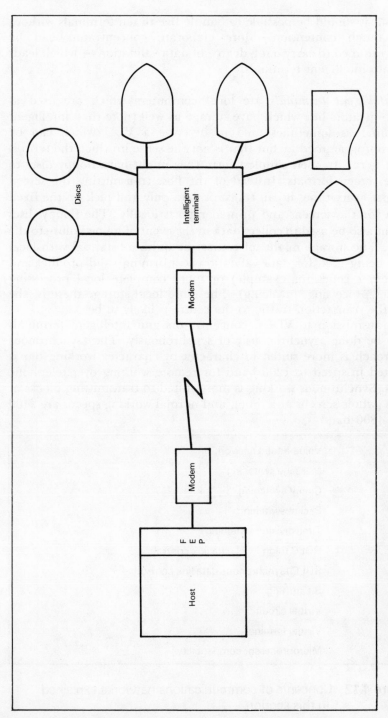

Figure 4.11 Using intelligent terminals to carry out local processing and line concentration

— but it should be possible to handle five to ten terminals without too much contention. More elaborate concentrators can be programmed to carry out a degree of data validation — which leads us into intelligent terminals.

Intelligent terminals are local computers which are used as concentrators but which have storage as well (note that 'intelligent terminal' is sometimes used to describe a VDU which can be microprogrammed — but that is not the sense in which the term is used here). In their simplest form they might have floppy discs to store screen formats. Instead of the host transmitting the screen format every time, it can transmit data only and pick up the fixed data for the screens and printed reports locally. The floppy discs might also be used to collect data in the event of a line failure to the host. The storage might, of course, be quite substantial with local files being used for data validation (confirming valid product and customer codes for example) or more complete local processing (order processing, invoicing). The more local storage there is, the less the transaction traffic to the centre is likely to be.

Transmission to VDUs, concentrators and intelligent terminals may be done asynchronously or synchronously. The asynchronous approach is more suited to character-by-character working but is limited in speed to 1200 baud for remote working over telephone lines. Synchronous working is more suited to transmitting blocks of data (whole screens at a time), and normal working speeds are 2400 and 4800 baud.

Value-added network

Message switching

Circuit switching

Packet switching

Time division switching

HDLC (high-level data link control)

SDLC (synchronous data link control)

Bit stuffing

Virtual circuit

Virtual terminal

Microprocessor compatibility

Figure 4.12   Concepts of communications networks explained
in this section

Communications networks

There are some applications which require fast access to a remote
database (say) but where the volume of traffic is low. For such
applications leased lines are unattractive because of the high fixed
cost in relation to traffic. Dial-up lines are unattractive because of
the lengthy connection time (typically fifteen seconds). At the
present time, and in the immediate future, there is no general
solution to this problem but there are developments underway.
Happily there are few business applications with these particular
requirements, so the limitation is of little practical difficulty for
most system designers.

One approach is to combine with other business users to share a
leased line. There are business organisations in the United States
which offer *value-added networks* in this way. They use the existing
communications services provided by the common carriers as the
base for additional (value added) services. Initially all
communications protocols on telephone lines were developed by
individual suppliers. The PTTs supplied the line but the method of
establishing the session and of sending the data was set by, for
example, IBM and other manufacturers. These methods fall into
the category of *private networks*. More recently the PTTs have been
trying to establish national and international protocols (in the same
way as telex is an international service) — to create *public networks*.

Public networks have the laudable aims of standardisation and
better utilisation of trunk lines. Standardisation suffers from the
problem of reconciling the needs of simple and demanding users,
while improving trunk utilisation is perhaps less relevant as the cost
of the trunk circuits continues to fall in relation to the local feeder
circuits. All this matters to the designer because the PTTs are likely
to introduce tariffs which force users in new directions — but
somewhat arbitrarily.

Most of the development effort of the PTTs is currently going into
digital switching. Digital switching can be subdivided into:

— message switching;
— packet switching;
— time division switching.

Message switching computers have existed for some time. They take
messages and send them on to the destination specified in the
message header. If a line is busy they store the message for later

transmission when the line is free. Message switching has the same lengthy connection time as *circuit switching* (as on a dial-up or leased line) so it is not the answer for intermittent transaction processing.

Packet switching involves breaking up messages into packets of typically 1024 bits. Every packet has its address header and is routed through the network from point to point with built-in error checking. The idea is that communication lines are often not used intensively and that many users can be served by a shared network with the advantages of lower individual costs.

Entry to the network is through packet switch exchanges which are being set up in all major centres. Access to these exchanges can be in one of two ways:

— messages are packeted by the user (either on a host computer or on a dedicated processor)
— character or block mode terminals are linked to a terminal processor (located at the exchange)

In the first case an international standard protocol (X25) has been established. In the second, a variety of existing synchronous and asynchronous terminals are supported. The link to the exchange can be in one of two ways:

— leased line, with no connection time
— dial-up line (with either a dedicated port at the exchange or a shared port)

It can be seen that packet switching, using leased lines, is a good answer to the problem of intermittent transaction processing, because computer-to-computer links are supported with a quick response, also computer-to-terminal links.

The disadvantages of packet switching are perhaps temporary (but none the less real at present):

— the initial investment is fairly high (software, processors, lines, modems) for low volumes — but will reduce
— for high volume traffic leased lines compare favourably in cost and are simpler
— coverage will not be geographically extensive until the mid-1980s (in UK and rest of Europe particularly)
— payment on a per packet basis does not favour existing protocols (2780 with an acknowledgement per block or polling) — users will be paying more for the control sequence than the data being sent

— if the network gets overloaded (as it may at peak times) packets
will be delayed with poor response time as a result

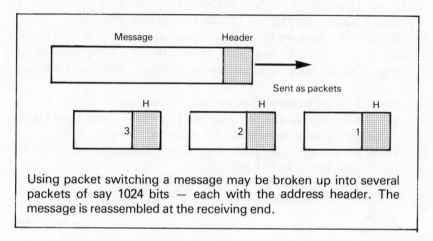

Using packet switching a message may be broken up into several
packets of say 1024 bits — each with the address header. The
message is reassembled at the receiving end.

Figure 4.13 Packet switching

Using packet switching it is not necessary to establish a physical
circuit — only a *virtual circuit*. A consequence is that two packets of
the same message may take different routes to their desination and
even arrive out of sequence. A job of the entry/exit nodes of the
network, therefore, is to ensure that all packets in a message are
reassembled into the correct sequence.

Time division switching is a technique which sends typically only
a character at a time. Circuits are established using specified time
intervals. Characters from a number of messages are thus
interleaved in the same sort of way that packets are interleaved in
packet switching and characters in TDM. The added complication
is that the circuits are switched as well, so a given message may be
interleaved with a different group of messages at every node of the
network. Time division switching is becoming more viable as the
cost of the necessary microprocessors falls and there is a view that it
will overtake packet switching — mainly because it does not delay
messages to the same extent as packet switching.

Because of the shifting nature of communications, the systems
designer has to observe two cardinal rules:

1. Separate the application modules from the communications
   modules within the system.
2. Only use thoroughly proven communications methods that
   demonstrably work.

By separating the application modules from the communications modules, it is possible to take advantage of future developments without affecting the whole system. By restricting the design to proven components the risk of failure is greatly reduced.

To help the designer identify the communication processes better, CCITT (Comité Consultatif International Téléphonique et Télégraphique) identify a number of protocol layers, or levels:

Level 1 is the physical link between processors.
Level 2 is the transmission protocol (e.g. 2780, HDLC or SDLC) including error detection and recovery.
Level 3 is the network protocol which selects the route through the network to a selected point.
Level 4 is the data access protocol which identifies the point to which the message must be sent.

CCITT term	IBM's SNA equivalent	DECNET equivalent
Level 4	Function management	Data access layer (DAP)
Level 3	Transmission control and path control	Network services protocol (NSP)
Level 2	SDLC	Digital data communication message protocol (DDCMP)

Figure 4.14 Equivalent terms of different suppliers

Figure 4.14 shows equivalent terms in current use and Figure 4.15 shows the way the levels operate conceptually.

HDLC stands for high-level data link control which is a bit-oriented protocol (*SDLC* or synchronous data link control is similar and used by IBM). Every message has a header and a trailer with a variable length text. There is cyclic redundancy checking in a similar way to 2780. The bit pattern '01111110' is the control character which indicates both the start and the end of a frame — to avoid problems should such a pattern occur in the text an additional '0' is inserted following *any* five consecutive '1' bits. Whenever five '1' bits are received followed by an '0' bit, the extra '0' is stripped off by the receiver. This way of achieving data transparency is known as bit stuffing.

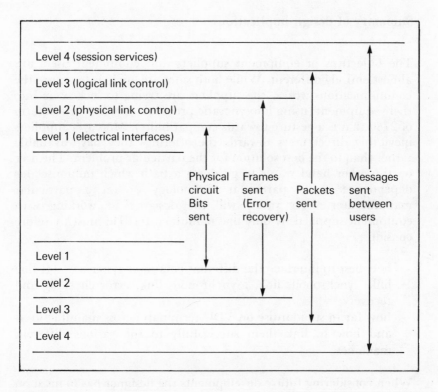

Figure 4.15 Separate levels of communication

An idea that looks attractive is to design all systems to interface to a common standard or *virtual terminal.* In practice such an interface proves to have too big an overhead (in protocol terms) for simple applications and is not powerful enough for complex, high-level applications. It is easier for the designer to use an established interface in a consistent way (and clearly separated from the application programs). For it is likely that future networks will provide an easy entry for established protocols. Alternatively the designer can use inexpensive microprocessors for code and protocol conversion. They are a form of dedicated front-end processor and can always be reprogrammed or replaced in the future to take advantage of new communications technology.

Summary of design implications

The objectives of equipment suppliers and equipment users are almost entirely different. While both sides are anxious to ensure the communications works, the suppliers are trying to lock users into their equipment (using idiosyncratic protocols together with a form of 2780 that is a gesture towards compatibility). Moreover suppliers inevitably direct users towards the offerings they have available rather than to the best solution for the particular problem. The user on the other hand wants to go down a path which minimises his dependence on a particular technology or on a particular manufacturer. Very rarely will the designer be working with equipment supplied by only one manufacturer. He must therefore consider:

— how best to interface the different computer systems — off-line link, synchronous link, asynchronous link, error checking and recovery;
— how far to standardise on VDU terminals across manufacturers and how to link them successfully to the various different machines.

When considering future developments the designer has to insist on reliable communications first, while being aware of current trends in communication methods. Separating the communication functions from the application programs is sound systems design and also isolates the areas which may be subject to future change.

5 File access methods

In Chapter 3 we saw the guidelines for determining the overall file strategy. We saw that ideally the files and processing should be close to the main user (the owner) for the application. Within an application it is possible to reduce the file organisation to one of three classes:

— centralised files;
— local files;
— part centralised and part local.

The purpose of this chapter is to look in detail at how these files might be organised. The chapter is organised into four parts:

1. Distributed files.
2. Transaction processing implications.
3. Data analysis and file design.
4. File access methods.

Distributed files

There is no particular merit in distributing inherently centralised files. We have seen that centralised files are needed for central applications and where many users need access to a common resource. If the file is split it becomes more difficult and more time-consuming to maintain. The point is illustrated in Figure 5.1. The distributed approach, in this case, means replicated files (all users need access to all the data) so a change in any one location must be followed by an update in all the others — much greater communications traffic than with the central approach. If the problem requires centralised files, then the best solution is to do as much local data validation as possible — and then to update a single copy of the file in the centre.

Going to the other extreme, there is no particular merit in centralising inherently local files. Centralisation in this case leads to unnecessary communications traffic and greater complexity, without reducing overall costs (for the reasons we saw in Chapter 3).

Both centralised and local extremes then reduce to a familiar design situation — on-line files but only one CPU to worry about at a time. The design problems occur when the application is mainly local — but with a need to access either the centre or other local files. The most familiar example is seen in depot stock control (of expensive items — cars for example), where there is a need to identify what is held at other depots to satisfy customer needs.

Figure 5.2 gives examples of applications which can be distributed and suggests the way they tend to fall. Branch banking,for example, is inherently centralised (because of central automated clearing primarily) although some processing can be done in the branch. It can be seen that **there are very few commercial applications where local and central processing are mixed in an interactive way.** The majority of applications do involve communications, but they are largely autonomous processes.

Interactive databases

Given the need for local files to interact, the system designer can choose three broad strategies — the central approach, the message switch approach and the local stand-alone approach.

The *central approach* at its extreme means holding all the files centrally even though most of the use is local. This approach would be adopted if, for example:

— no local hardware exists and this is a relatively small application;
— the interaction *between* sites is a high proportion of all transactions.

A variation on the central approach would be to update central files overnight and for these central files to be available for interrogation. The local application would have only one place to look for the data. The approach is straightforward — but of course the files are only correct to the previous night. It would be possible,

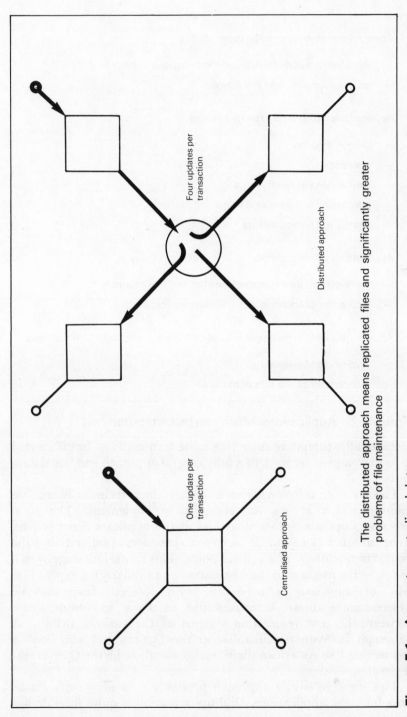

Figure 5.1   Access to centralised data

Applications which tend to be local

- stock control at multiple locations (inexpensive items)
- order-processing for local depots

Applications which tend to be centralised

- branch banking
- insurance
- central (single) stock points
- purchasing and purchase ledger
- payroll and personnel files

Applications which are mixed — in an interactive way

- stock control (of expensive items) at multiple locations
- local order-processing with central credit control

Applications which can be either local or central — depending on business

- invoicing and sales ledger
- standard times and bills of material

Figure 5.2   Applications which can be distributed

theoretically, to update these files more frequently — but if carried to its extreme we are back to a fully central approach with local data entry.

The *message switch approach* tends to be a technically feasible solution which is not too complex to implement. The local processors operate autonomously — if the application needs data from another location it sends a message, prefixed by the destination address, to a central point. This central message switch re-routes the message to the destination and similarly the reply. This type of approach is used by SITA (Société Internationale Télécommunications Aeronautiques) in Paris to communicate between the seat reservation systems of the various airlines. A passenger in Sydney, Australia, at the Qantas desk can book a connecting Pan American flight in this way through the Qantas seat reservation system.

This message switch approach probably does not justify leased lines for most applications. Dial-up operation is quite feasible but delays of at least thirty seconds will be caused while the connections are being made (not, one hopes, a further thirty seconds for the return message). The approach also presupposes knowledge of where to go to get the data — presumably starting at the nearest locations.

The *local stand-alone approach* is very cost-effective if the enquiry traffic is infrequent. At its simplest it involves no direct communication between local computers — it is possible to telephone the stock office in the other depot just like another customer. Alternatively one local computer can dial another directly (avoiding the need for a message switch) making a connection which lasts the duration of the dialogue.

In summary, distributed files present few new or complex problems for the great majority of commercial applications. There is little advantage in splitting up an inherently centralised system of files (except to improve local validation) and few applications require local files to interact with each other (almost by definition).

Transaction processing considerations

In a transaction-processing or on-line system it is the random access device which becomes the limiting factor — sooner or later. Processor power will be adequate for a commercial mix of jobs (unless a paging approach is used by the operating system — which then has the overhead of base address registers for every page). Even the 64k address space limitation (for eight and sixteen bit minicomputers) is not a practical handicap. On-line systems thrive on smallish programs which can service many users in memory at once. Big programs lead to fewer users in main memory which leads to more swapping. Swapping large programs takes a long time (typically 150 msecs to swap a 64k program out to disc and in), so reducing program size has cumulative benefits.

Quite apart from program swapping, on-line systems place greater demands on the disc than do batch systems. There are several reasons for this:

1. All files tend to be held on disc (magnetic tape, if available, is used for log files).
2. All main files have to be accessed randomly, with the overhead of indexes (in batch processing one file at least is sequential).
3. The work is subject to peak demands which must be serviced at acceptable speed.

There is thus a need to minimise disc activity in the interests of the specific application and of the whole system.

Multiple-update protection

A further problem arises when two users wish to update the same record. Suppose for example that operator A wishes to take three of an item out of stock and operator B wishes to take one of the same item out of stock. We risk the situation shown in Figure 5.3 — instead of reducing the stock by four it is only reduced by one.

The solution varies from system to system but involves 'lock-out' at one or more of the following levels:

— file lock-out;
— record lock-out;
— logical page lock-out.

File lock-out

Files can be opened for read only, write only, single-user update and multi-user update. Flags are set to indicate the file status and these flags are inspected before every input/output request is executed (and before the file is first opened). So if a user opens a file in read-only mode, then any write instructions in such a program are trapped as errors.

With a minicomputer there is no great problem — because the main operating system and the transaction-processing operating system generally are the same. On a traditional mainframe it is not enough to hold this information in the transaction-processing system — there would be no lock-out to batch programs running at the same time. There thus need to be two sets of flags, and if the mainframe does not provide this protection it has to be built in. While one user is doing an update (read record, modify, write back), it is theoretically.possible to lock the whole file out to other users. Such an approach is easy to implement but it would slow down order processing (for example) to little more than the speed of one screen. There has to be a way of locking only part of the file at a time (preferably only the record we are working on).

Record lock-out

At first sight, record lock-out looks the most attractive method. In fact it is technically difficult to implement with considerable software and disc-accessing overheads. The problem is illustrated in

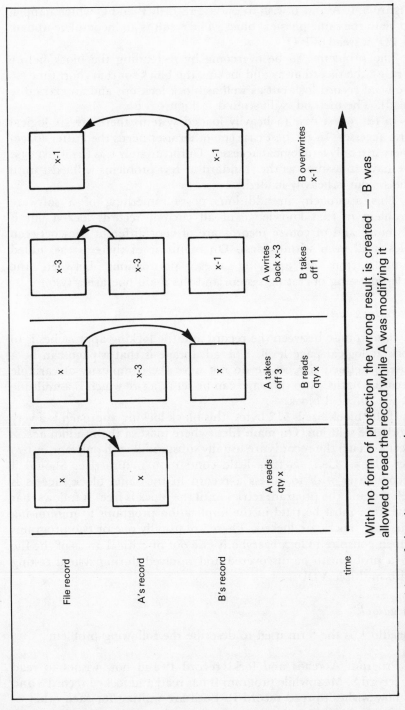

Figure 5.3 Problem of simultaneous update

Figure 5.4. A and B wish to update records P and Q which happen to be in the same physical block. The result is an incomplete update — PQ′ instead of P′Q′.

The problem can be overcome by re-reading the block before writing the record away and locking the block for that short time (so we need record lock-out as well as block lock-out and an extra disc read). The method is illustrated in Figure 5.5.

In the worst case (a heavily loaded system) there are six logical disc accesses. In the best case (no other user needs the buffer space) there are only two logical accesses. Unfortunately it is the worst case we have to assume as the standard as few problems will exist until the system is heavily loaded.

This approach, in addition, poses something of a software problem in that knowledge of all current records locked out is required and of course records are of very different sizes between files (and even within files). On mainframes there is the added complication of applying these permissions between the teleprocessing operating system and the main operating system.

Page lock-out

A compromise between the record and file locking approaches is to lock at logical page level. The advantage is that a page can be a (user-) defined size, so we do not have the complexity of variable record lengths. Also the page can be set at a size which is a multiple of the physical block.

If the block size is 512 bytes, this block locking approach is a very workable solution. On main files (where most of the random access needs occur) the records are usually substantial with only one or two per block. There is thus little contention in practice. Should a second user wish to access a record in the same block, access is refused and the program retries until the block is free. It follows that attention must be paid in the application programs to minimising the time blocks are locked. There are usually one or two programs which conspire to lock everybody else out of critical areas of the file — a problem to be discovered and resolved during system testing with multiple VDUs.

Deadlock

Deadlock is the term used to describe the following problem:

Program A reads and locks record P and now wishes to read record S. Meanwhile program B has read and locked record S and now wishes to read record P. Both are waiting for each other.

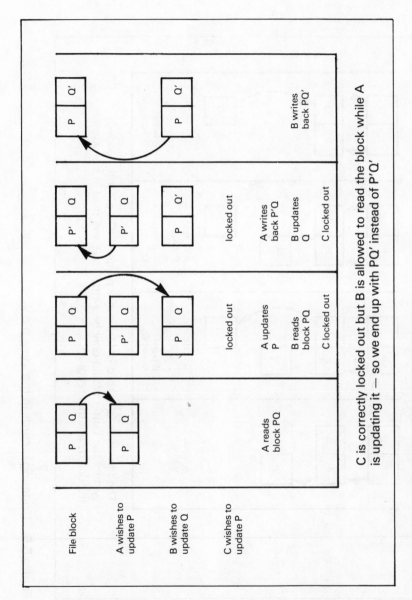

C is correctly locked out but B is allowed to read the block while A is updating it — so we end up with PQ' instead of P'Q'

Figure 5.4   The problem of lockout at record level

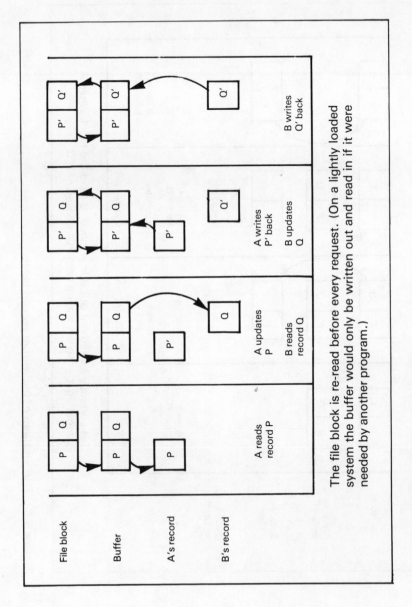

The file block is re-read before every request. (On a lightly loaded system the buffer would only be written out and read in if it were needed by another program.)

Figure 5.5   Updating records in the same block

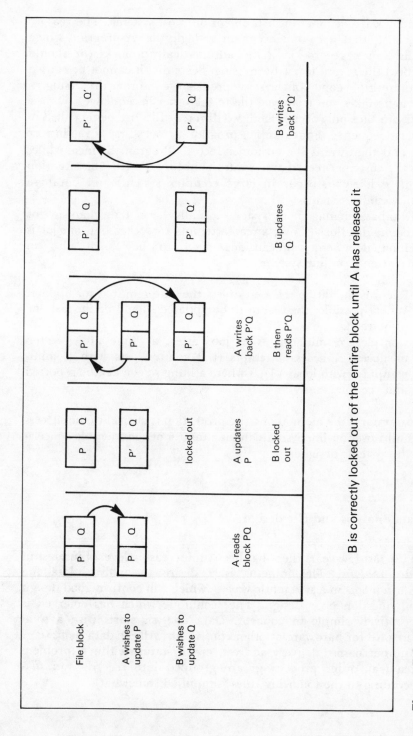

Figure 5.6   Lockout at block level

Deadlock is not much of a problem on most systems. The reasons are, first, that it cannot occur on a single file. A program which reads a new record on a file automatically unlocks (or should unlock) the record it has been using. Secondly, it cannot be caused from multiple copies of the same program, e.g. order processing — the logic takes you from one file to the other in sequence.

It can thus only occur when two different files are being called in reverse sequence. For example, program A looks first at the history file and then wants the customer record. Program B, meanwhile, has the customer record and wants the history record. This situation is more likely to occur in large complex systems and database management systems.

Database management systems usually have a mechanism for detecting deadlock (if over x read attempts are locked out, one job is terminated). Some precautions need to be taken also in conventional on-line systems:

1. Records should be released unless they are required for update.
2. Where possible, the record to be updated should be the last one to be read.
3. Consider terminating the job after a 'time-out' — ten unsuccessful access attempts (this matters less with a mini-computer with local VDUs where a hung screen can be reported and rectified easily).

In summary, the method of write protection is critical to the success of multi-user on-line systems and is a matter of considerable concern to the systems designer.

Data analysis and file design

In the last few years there has been an increasing level of interest in *data analysis*. The impetus is a desire to analyse data file requirements in a systematic way — which will confirm good design and question poor design. The technique which has emerged is deceptively simple in concept. Data analysis starts with a total disregard for hardware or other constraints. All the data *items* (e.g. customer name, delivery address, credit status) within a problem area (say order processing) are grouped into *records* and *files* according to the following rules (simplified somewhat):

1. Within a file all records are of the same type — there are no repeating groups.
2. Every item within a record depends on the key to that record.
3. Apart from their common key, items within a record are not related in any way.

A file which satisfies all three of these rules is said to be in third normal form (TNF). A file which satisfies only the first rule is said to be in first normal form; similarly for second normal form. The concept of analysing files into their basic (normal) form is illustrated by an order-processing example. The main data items are shown in Figure 5.7. Organising the files into third normal form leads to the files in Figure 5.8. Most of the files are as expected except the open-order file where the variable number of order items is split from the order header/trailer.

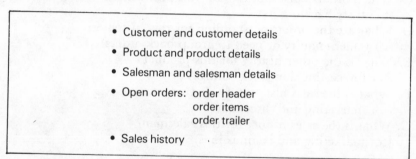

Figure 5.7   Order processing data items

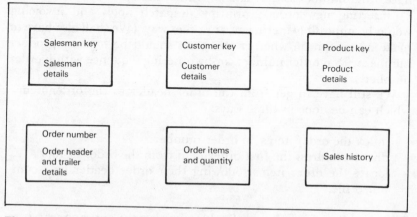

Figure 5.8   TNF files for order processing

The files are clearly separated into logical entities which now need to be refined further:

— what additional files/indexes are needed to satisfy the business need?
— what files can be combined sensibly to improve efficiency?

The operational need is to be able to answer the following classes of question:

A. What are the items within this order and their status?
   (for despatch, invoicing and enquiry)
B. How many orders are outstanding for this product?
   (for forecasting and reordering)
C. Which orders outstanding want this product?
   (to satisfy back orders)
D. What are the orders outstanding for this customer?
   (customer enquiry or need to group back orders)
E. What is the order history for this product?
   (for forecasting and stock control)
F. What is the sales history for this customer?
   (for marketing and discount)
G. What is the sales history for this salesman?
   (for marketing and commissions)

In order of importance, 'A' is top because it is the high-volume routine operational need. It follows that the order item file must have order number as the main key rather than product or customer — inserting new orders, printing despatch notes and invoicing would be impossibly inefficient any other way. (We shall also have to make a decision on whether the items should be held by product number within order number, or by ordering sequence within order number.)

We still have to get from the order header to the order items, which can be done in three ways:

— index the order items on order number;
— directly address the first order item from the order header;
— locate the order items following their order header in a combined file.

The combined file is not difficult to implement and one way is to group together order items in larger records which are the same size as the order header. So, for example, an order header record of 256

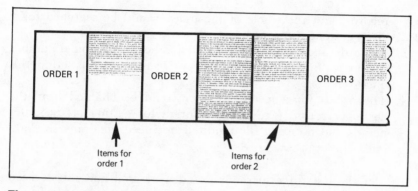

Figure 5.9 Organisation of open order file

bytes might be followed by one or more 256-byte records containing up to sixteen order items (sixteen bytes long) in each.

To answer question 'B' (the total orders outstanding for a product), we can either search all the order items accumulating the total, chain through them from the product record or hold the quantity outstanding as an additional item on the product file. The first two approaches would again be too inefficient in most applications, so there are good practical reasons for the third. In fact the product file can hold a series of subtotals in this way (back orders, forward orders by month) to suit the application.

To answer question 'C' (which orders outstanding require this product?) requires us to go into the detail of question 'B'. At first sight we must either search the whole open-order file or chain through it from the product record. But the requirement is to fulfil back orders. In practice, back orders are either actioned directly in the warehouse (from copies of the despatch note) or they are allocated by the computer in a batch run (we want to combine despatches where possible). The computer run can take place at the end of the day after the day's receipts have been input. Happily the orders will be processed in order number sequence so the earliest will get priority — which will suit most problems of this nature.

Question 'D' is concerned with identifying all the orders outstanding for this customer. This requirement could be satisfied in a number of ways:

1. The orders could be held by customer (very inefficient for inserting new orders and we will need two indexes for the file — one by customer, the other by order number).
2. The order index could be extended to include customer numbers (the lowest index level would be one-for-one with the data

records, and the whole of the index would be searched for a given customer's orders).
3. The order index could be inverted and held by customer number (an extra file to maintain but well-suited to answering this question).
4. The orders for a given customer could be chained from the customer record (the fastest solution for getting at the order details and no extra file required but needs chaining software and utilities).

Any of the last three methods would work well and the decision depends to a large degree on the file management software available. If we select the third solution we have now reached the decisions in Figure 5.10.

Customer file:	*key* customer code,	need to access randomly and sequentially, fixed length records
Product file:	*key* product code,	need to access randomly and sequentially, fixed length records
Open order file:	*key* order number,	need to access randomly and sequentially. Order header and order items combined in one file
Customer index:		index to customer file
Product index:		index to product file
Order index:		index to open order file
Customer/order index:		intersection of customer and order files

Figure 5.10   Decisions on file structure

We will return to the method of indexing once we have looked at the remaining three requirements. Question 'E' is concerned with the order history for this product for forecasting and stock control. What is required is the order pattern over a number of recent periods — we are not concerned with individual orders. One approach would be to hold orders on a month-by-month basis for this year and last year — a maximum of twenty-four monthly figures per product. These fields, logically, should be held in the product file as they depend on the product key.

Question 'F' is concerned with the sales history for this customer. If we are only interested in sales value then monthly figures can be held in the customer record. If a deeper analysis is required, for example, of sales to each customer by product group, then a periodic batch analysis run would be appropriate. All the invoiced items in the period would be sorted by product group within customer and the analysis tabulated as well as being written to a history file.

Question 'G' is concerned with the sales history for a given salesman, both for marketing and for commission purposes. Again the analysis can be held as a single figure per month on the salesman file or a more comprehensive analysis prepared during a batch processing run.

Up to now we have only needed to access the product and customer files randomly. In practice we will wish to access them sequentially as well (i.e. the branches of a particular customer need to be grouped together, products need to be printed in a consistent and logical way). Here are the ways of achieving both sequential and random access:

1. Hold the file sequentially, gain random access through an index (e.g. index sequential access method).
2. Use a hash-random algorithm for accessing the data record directly, keep a separate file of keys in sequential sequence (sequential index).
3. Hold the file randomly, keep several separate files of keys in as many sequences as is necessary.
4. Hold the file randomly and be prepared to sort the file before printing reports.

The most suitable method is a balance of efficiency during on-line processing (desire for few accesses) and inserting records (every extra index means additional overheads) and batch processing efficiency (often out-of-hours working). If the index sequential access method is chosen, the final organisation is as shown in Figure 5.10.

In summary, data analysis consists of first grouping data items into records so that:

— there are no repeating groups;
— all items depend on the key;
— items are only related by the key.

The result will tend to consist of a number of main files (e.g. product, customer, salesman) and a number of transaction files (open order file, sales ledger transactions, sales history).

The second step is to organise and cross index the files so that:

— daily operation is efficient;
— enquiries can be actioned efficiently;
— periodic runs are adequately efficient;
— the result is not too complex.

The second step is more properly File Design rather than Data Analysis and some authorities advocate keeping the two steps very distinct. Practical experience, however, suggests that the two processes must be closely linked if an over-theoretical (and inappropriate) solution is to be avoided. For example, both need to be carried out before deciding on a database management system.

Data Analysis then is a useful technique to start off the file design process, but it is no substitute for a first class analyst with detailed knowledge of the business area.

File access methods

There is no easy solution to the problem of file access efficiency, because of the nature of the problem:

1. Main file records tend to be large; they have relatively few insertions and deletions but amendments are frequent.
2. Transaction records tend to be small; they have constant insertions and deletions but amendments are generally not allowed.
3. Main file records tend to be accessed from a single key; transaction records may be accessed by many keys.

The table in Figure 5.11 compares some of the main methods of organising files against four criteria:

— efficiency of inserting new records;
— random access efficiency;
— sequential access efficiency;
— file integrity and recovery.

The methods are compared on a five-point scale (excellent, very good, good, fair and poor). The main reasons for these value judgements are discussed in the remainder of this chapter.

Organisation	Inserting new records efficiency	Random access efficiency	Sequential access efficiency	File integrity and recovery
Sequential	Not possible	Not possible	Excellent	Excellent
Relative	Very good	Excellent	Not applicable	Fair
Index sequential	Poor	Good	Very good	Good
B-tree	Poor	Good	Good	Fair
Hash random (IAM)	Good	Very good	Needs sort	Fair
Inverted	Very poor	Good	Good	Good
Chained	Fair	Poor	Good	Poor
Database		varies — see text		

Figure 5.11 File organisation methods compared

Sequential organisation

Sequential files are well understood and may be held on tape or disc. They are suitable for history files, log files and situations where new records can be added to the end of the file. They can only be used for random access if they are either very short (effectively a table) or if enquiries are few and a delay is acceptable.

Relative organisation

Relative files (or random files) are accessed directly 'relative' to their start address — in the same way as a table is addressed. The file is treated as a number of fixed length records numbered sequentially from 1 to the end of the file. It is possible to get any record by specifying the record number — a system of pigeon holes in fact. Adding new records and accessing them directly is straightforward and efficient. Sequential reading is generally not applicable.

Index sequential organisation

The index sequential access method (ISAM) is the most widely-used method of combining random and sequential access to files. The method is illustrated in Figure 5.12.

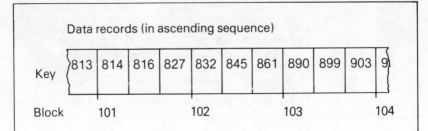

Data records (in ascending sequence)

Key: 813 | 814 | 816 | 827 | 832 | 845 | 861 | 890 | 899 | 903 | 9

Block: 101 · 102 · 103 · 104

Fine index

highest key in block

```
827 – 101
861 – 102
903 – 103
```

block   003

Coarse index

highest key in block

```
 402 – 001
 813 – 002
1333 – 003
```

block   000

If the record with key 845 is required:

- the coarse index (usually in memory) shows that block 003 contains the relevant fine index

- inspection of block 003 (following a disc access) shows that block 102 contains the relevant record

- reading block 102 (a second disc access) makes the record available for processing

Figure 5.12   Index sequential access method

The ISAM method is well suited to main files but not to transaction files. The problem with transaction files arises because of the inefficiency caused by adding any volume of new transactions. In practice new transactions are not evenly spread across the file — they tend to bunch causing overflow and further overflow. At best, four disc accesses are required and, at worst, many more. The table in Figure 5.13 shows how many accesses are required for different key lengths and blocking factors.

Key length (bytes)	Minimum number of accesses	Records per 512-byte block			
		1	2	4	8
5	3	5329	10658	21316	42632
	4	over 32000	64000	128000	256000
10	3	1764	3528	7056	14112
	4	over 32000	64000	128000	256000
15	3	900	1800	3600	7200
	4	27000	54000	108000	216000
20	3	529	1058	2116	4232
	4	12167	24334	48668	97336
25	4	5832	11664	23328	46656
30	4	3375	6750	13500	27000

This table shows the minimum number of disc accesses required for different key sizes and blocking factors — assuming 512-byte physical blocks. Most main files (substantial records and lengthy keys) will need four disc accesses.

Figure 5.13 Disc accesses required with ISAM organisation

Suppose for example that there are two data records in a 512-byte block. Suppose further that the key is ten characters long, then the index blocks will be organised with forty-two keys to the block (12 × 42 = 504 — the twelve characters being the 10-byte key plus 2-byte block address):

— the coarse index can address up to forty-two blocks;
— the next index can address up to 1764 blocks (42 × 42);
— the fine index can address up to 74088 blocks, i.e. 148176 records (in practice, many minicomputers can address a maximum of 32767 blocks in any file).

B-tree organisation

The *B-tree* organisation structure is a method of organising records in a way that is self-indexing. The method is illustrated in Figure 5.14 for a B-tree of order 2. In a tree of order 'm' there are at least m and at most 2m records in a logical block.

The approach is attractive because:

— records can be read sequentially fairly efficiently;
— records can be read randomly efficiently;
— programming is elegant (and recursive).

The technique is not suited to data records in a multi-user environment. Adding a new record may cause block overflow, which is handled by dividing the block into two. The records are thus unstable and there is no guarantee that records will be in the same place for an update following a read. (It is also inefficient in its use of space.) It can, however, be used for organising index records provided precautions are taken to lock the index during record insertion/deletion.

Hash random methods

We have seen that the index sequential access method has two disadvantages for on-line working. The first is the relatively high number of disc accesses required to locate a record (typically four reads). The second is the degradation in performance that occurs if a substantial number of new records are added to the file.

A way of getting over the first problem is to hold the record according to some permutation of the access key. In practice this 'hash/random' approach has three disadvantages:

— the records are no longer sequential;
— loading/reorganising the file is time-consuming;
— no hash/random algorithm exists which spreads keys evenly and thinly (i.e. where there are very few records in the physical block), so records 'bunch' and overflow is inevitable.

nor does it solve the problem of inserting new records.

There is an ingenious variation, which is known as IAM or indexed access method. In this method the data file can be held in any sequence — the key (with a pointer to the data record) is held in a second file which is known as the index file. The randomising algorithm calculates the position of the key in the index file —

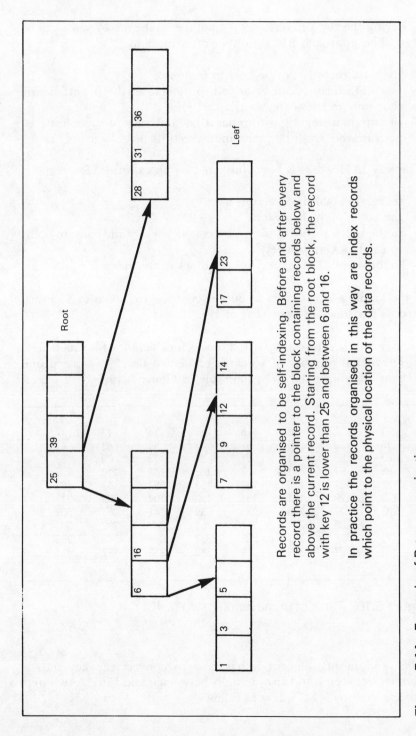

Records are organised to be self-indexing. Before and after every record there is a pointer to the block containing records below and above the current record. Starting from the root block, the record with key 12 is lower than 25 and between 6 and 16.

In practice the records organised in this way are index records which point to the physical location of the data records.

Figure 5.14 Example of B-tree organisation

retrieving the key also retrieves the pointer so the data record can be read. The approach has a number of attractions:

— the data records can be held in sequence;
— new data records can be added to the end of the file efficiently (but only in the sequence they arise);
— the randomising algorithm has a good chance of succeeding — because there will be many index records per block.

The way IAM works is best illustrated by an example. Suppose:

— there are 5000 data records and
— the key is eight bytes long
— so the index record is twelve bytes (the key + four bytes to point to the block and offset)
— so there are 42 index records per block in the index file (512/12).

If the loading factor is set at 80 per cent we are down to 33 index records per block (80 per cent of 42):

— we need therefore at least 152 blocks for the index file (5000/33);
— the actual number of blocks is chosen to be 157 — the prime number above 152 from the table in Figure 5.15.

1	2	3	5	7	11	13	17
19	23	29	31	37	41	43	47
53	59	61	67	71	73	79	83
89	97	101	103	107	109	113	127
131	137	139	149	151	157	163	167
173	179	181	191	193	197	199	211
223	227	229	233	239	241	251	257
263	269	271	277	281	283	293	307
311	313	317	331	337	347	349	353
359	367	373	379	383	389	397	401

Figure 5.15   Table of prime numbers up to 401

The randomising algorithm has now to convert the key into a number between 1 and 157 (actually between 0 and 156). A two-step process used by DEC works as follows:

— In step one, all the digits in odd positions (1, 3, 5, 7, etc.) are multiplied by 516 and added to the sum of the even positions multiplied by 2;
— the result is divided by 157 and the remainder gives the block number where the index record is to be found.

For example, the eight-digit key might be 30785146:

— multiply the odd positions by 516 and sum them:
$(3 + 7 + 5 + 4) \times 516 = 9804$;

— multiply the even positions by 2 and sum them:
$(0 + 8 + 1 + 6) \times 2 = 30$;

— divide the sum of the two (9834) by 157 to get remainder 100.

Access to the hundredth block should give the key, together with its four-byte pointer to the data record. In most cases the data record will be accessed in two disc reads. Should the index block be full the overflow block is calculated by adding a second (different) prime number to the current block number (100 in this case) and taking the result mod 157.

The process is repeated until the block containing the key is found. To avoid all overflow ending in the same place, the second prime is chosen from one of five primes (by taking the hashing value mod 5). So long as the second prime is different from the first, every block in the table will be visited before going back to the original block.

The hashing algorithm described is simple and can be applied efficiently to variable length keys which may be numeric or non-numeric — the character is treated as a binary value.

Some test results will show how effective the algorithm is on two actual files. The two files are:

1. *Customer file* which contains 4216 data records. Actually 2108 records, each of which is duplicated. One has a numeric key, the other has an alphabetic short name and town code. In both cases the key is twelve characters long leading to twenty-five keys per index block (80 per cent filled).
2. *Outstanding orders file* which contains 10009 data records. The key is thirty charcters long (including customer number, date of order, date of delivery, warehouse and serial number) leading to twelve keys per index block.

The four randomising algorithms used in the test were:

1. Multiplying successive characters by their position (I) and summing them — the weights are thus 1, 2, 3, 4, 5, 6, etc.
2. Multiplying successive characters by (2I-1) and summing them — the weights are thus 1, 3, 5, 7, 9, 11, etc. (missing out multiples of 2).
3. Multiplying successive characters by (2I-1) but missing out also multiples of three — the weights are thus 5, 7, 11, 13, 17, 19, etc. (all primes so far).
4. Use the IAM method, multiply alternate characters by 516 and 2 and sum them.

The results when the index was generated for the customer file of 4216 records were as follows:

Method	Elapsed time mins	CPU time mins	No of overflow keys	No of overflow accesses
1. (I)	16.88	5.29	99	100
2. (2I-1)	16.52	5.41	40	45
3. (2I-1) not mod 3	16.40	5.28	15	15
4. IAM	16.18	4.66	65	66

All methods are seen to have very few overflows. Method 3 has fewest disc accesses and a fairly good CPU time. Method 4 has an acceptable number of disc accesses and the best throughput.

The results when generating the index for the outstanding orders file were as follows:

Method	Elapsed time mins	CPU time mins	No of overflow keys	No of overflow accesses
1. (I)	33.4	15.7	1482	3389
2. (2I-1)	31.2	14.8	381	498
3. (2I-1) not mod 3	30.8	14.5	339	473
4. IAM	36.6	15.9	3254	8326

Here we see that method 3 comes out best on all counts — method 4 is worst on all counts. The results were so bad that a special fifth run was carried out which merely took the serial number in the key, and reversed it as the hashing value. The results were, as expected, good:

5. Serial No   26.3   9.7   554   733

Using knowledge of a key can always produce a good result but such an approach is not acceptable in most commercial environments where a single copy of the file access software must be used for all files.

Following these tests the installation decided to stay with the IAM method. Method 3 was superior, but the cost of changing was not worth the effort for just one file which was performing badly. In any case the 'bad' file still only needed an average of 2.83 accesses per data record (ISAM on the same file would have needed over five).

Various other algorithms were tested and rejected because they took too much calculation time or because they were ineffective (some had over 26000 overflow accesses).

There is no hashing algorithm which is going to be successful in every situation but methods 3 and 4 above seem to be simple and effective starters. On large files with long keys the system designer should carry out simulations to ensure gross inefficiency is avoided.

Inverted files

The inverted file organisation is conceptually similar to IAM — in the sense that the index file is separate from the data file and may be in quite a different sequence. The difference with IAM is that the index file is itself held as an index sequential file.

If a file is fully inverted, then an index is held for all possible keys. The index record in each case consists of the selected key and the physical data record address (often the primary key rather than the physical address).

The inverted approach is an effective way of accessing a file from different keys but it has some disadvantages:

— sequential reading is not efficient;
— inserting records is very slow because several indexes have to be updated;
— inserting records may also be inefficient if the data records are held in a logical sequence (same problem as ISAM).

Chained file organisation

Record chaining allows transaction records to be linked to a master record, which may be part of a different file. There is usually a free record chain which is used to allocate space for new records which are then linked into their appropriate chains. The approach is flexible because chains can point forwards and backwards; there can also be more than one chain through a record (allowing it to be accessed from different directions). The main problem is inefficiency. To read a chain sequentially, at worst, requires a disc access per record in the chain — to find a particular record, at worst, means going right round the chain until it is found. There are a number of ways of reducing this inefficiency:

— periodically reorganise the records so they are physically sequential (in the most-used sequence) — only new records are out of place;
— point to the end of the chain from the master record — so new records can be added without a complete circuit (in general there must be forward and backward pointers in all chains);
— locate the records according to a randomising algorithm — so they can be accessed directly as well as being read sequentially via the chain (the approach used in the IDS database).

Subsidiary problems of chaining include extra disc space used (for the chains) and problems of file integrity. A total of the transaction records should be held in the master record and utilities run regularly to verify all the chains. The more the chains that exist, the more difficult and time-consuming it is to verify the integrity of the file and to recover from failure.

Database management systems

A database is a collection of data which is to be shared by many different applications. A database management system (DBMS) defines the way the data is held and provides programs to allow:

— data sharing;
— data integrity;
— security of data;
— transparency of organisation to the application program.

The element which describes the way the data is organised and its

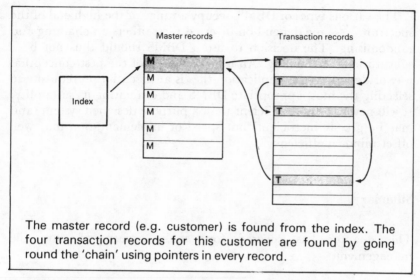

The master record (e.g. customer) is found from the index. The four transaction records for this customer are found by going round the 'chain' using pointers in every record.

Figure 5.16   Master records with chained transactions

validation rules is known as the *schema*. The element which describes the way the data appears to a particular application is known as the *sub-schema*.

Database management systems (DBMS) are at one end of a spectrum of the file access methods (see Figure 5.17). At the low end of the spectrum it is theoretically possible for users to write their own input/output routines, in assembler, and their own device drivers. Even though the approach is likely to be efficient, there are few users who would attempt it — too much delay and risk without a good enough playback. Access methods such as ISAM are somewhere in the middle of the spectrum.

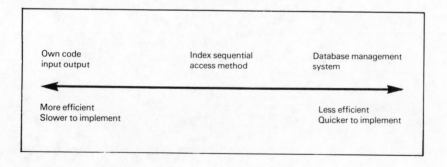

Figure 5.17   Spectrum of file access methods

The various types of DBMS occupy a range at the high end of the spectrum — some depend on inverted files, others on chaining and randomising. The decision to use a DBMS should thus not be a substitution for thinking. An understanding of the best conceptual way of designing the application files is an essential prerequisite to selecting the most appropriate DBMS and evaluating its suitability. It will never be more efficient than a purpose designed system (and may be grossly inefficient) but speed of implementation may well offset minor inefficiency.

Summary

This chapter has covered four main aspects of data file management:

1. Distributed files are seen to be more of a theoretical problem than a practical one.
2. Successful transaction processing relies on an effective means of record lock-out (although in practice lock-out is not just at record level).
3. Data analysis is a systematic way of analysing file structures as a first step in the file design process.
4. A variety of file access methods exists, no one of which is right in all situations.

For medium to high-volume transaction-processing systems these are the areas the system designer is concerned with.

6 Deciding the hardware strategy

Selecting equipment to satisfy the business need requires a trade-off between hardware performance and software availability; between a proliferation of 'ideal' solutions and the rigidity of a single solution. This chapter identifies the characteristics of mainframe, mini and microcomputers as a basis for deciding a hardware strategy. The topics covered include:

— hardware overview;
— operating system overview;
— review of essential basic software;
— choice of programming language;
— custom-built hardware;
— guidelines for choosing the hardware.

Hardware overview

The dividing line between classes of computers is fading as mini and microcomputers grow in power. We will distinguish mainframe, mini and microcomputers as much by the way they are used as by their architecture.

Mainframe computers we define as multi-user systems with powerful batch-processing capability and large user address space.

Minicomputers we define as multi-user interactive systems in which each user can have up to 64k bytes of address space (the 16-bit address limitation).

Microcomputers we define as single-user, interactive systems with up to 64k bytes of memory.

We will now go on to examine the hardware architecture of each class in turn.

Mainframe architecture

A typical modern mainframe architecture is illustrated in Figure 6.1.

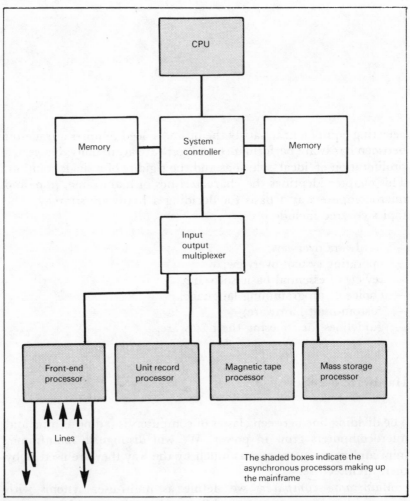

Figure 6.1   Example of mainframe architecture

The mainframe is in fact made up of several active processors which are working asynchronously. The CPU is available at several different speeds, manipulating between 32 and 96 bits at a time in decimal, packed decimal and floating point modes. User programs operate with zero-relative addresses and execute within boundaries set in the base address register. To obtain higher throughput, techniques are used such as:

— cache memory (very fast random access memory of a few thousand words located in the processor — so the processor can fetch a whole block of instructions from main memory rather than one at a time);
— look ahead (the next instruction is decoded while the current instruction is being executed);
— interleaved memory (memory cycles are overlapped to obtain higher overall throughput).

The system controller is passive and handles all accesses to the main memory modules. It resolves conflicts in favour of the input/output multiplexer. Memory cycle time is of the order of 500 to 750 nanoseconds per access (of 32 to 96 bits at a time) and on larger machines error detection and correction logic is included.

The input/output multiplexer allows a peak data transfer rate of five million bytes per second or more from peripherals directly to memory. Once the transfer is initiated the processor is free to continue with other work. The peripheral processors (unit record processor, magnetic tape processor and mass storage processor) act as intelligent controllers, for example overlapping seeks on multiple disc drives. More elaborate mass storage processors can also contain file management software.

The front-end processor is a specialist communications handler. It is designed to handle a variety of lines and speeds using a range of communications protocols. Because it operates independently and asynchronously of the rest of the mainframe, it removes the (considerable) burden of network and communications management from the CPU.

Mainframes started as a single processor with a single block of memory. To improve throughput there is an increasing move to functional modules which separate applications processing from communications handling and database management. The modular design and asynchronous operation means a range of processing power is available with relatively smooth growth to multiple processor configurations.

Minicomputer architecture

A typical minicomputer architecture is illustrated in Figure 6.2. The processor, memory and peripherals communicate via a high-speed data highway. On the PDP-11 range of minicomputers the data highway is known as the Unibus and has 56 lines for the transfer of data, address and control signals.

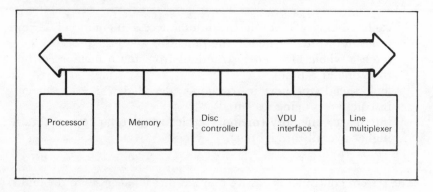

Figure 6.2   The unibus concept

The form of communications is the same for all devices on the Unibus. Every device is assigned an address on the bus so peripherals are addressed as if they are memory locations. This approach simplifies the instruction set (there are no special input/output instructions), allows instructions to manipulate data in the peripheral device registers and makes it easier to add 'unusual' devices to the computer.

In addition to a 'bus' based structure, minicomputers have most of the following features:

— 16-bit word allowing direct addressing of 64k 8-bit bytes with both word and byte processing;
— asynchronous operation allowing system components to run at their highest speed. Replacement with faster components improves the speed without affecting other hardware and software;
— direct memory access (DMA) from fast peripherals to memory once the transfer is initiated by the processor;
— stack processing making it easier to handle subroutines, re-entrant code and interrupts;
— automatic priority interrupt at several levels. Every device is assigned a priority (at several different levels) and within a single

level devices physically closer to the CPU have higher priority;
— hardware interrupt without device polling. When a device gets control it sends the processor a unique memory address containing a new program counter (PC) and program status (PS) word. The old PC and PS are stored on the stack, the new PC and PS (known as the interrupt vector) is loaded and the interrupt service routine initiated automatically;
— a power fail service routine is initiated whenever the power supply falls outside specified limits. When power is restored, the machine restarts in the state prior to power failure — but volatile memory is lost.

In practice it is possible to overload the bus with individual slow peripherals. A line multiplexer with its own buffer can service typically sixteen lines and send data transfers at high speed directly to memory. Sixteen individual interfaces provide much more of a load on the bus (and the processor) and characters can get lost when higher priority devices get control. Even using multiplexers there is a practical limit of sixteen or so VDUs attached to a single bus. The larger minicomputers now have a high-speed bus in addition to the standard bus (see Figure 6.3) with memory accessible from both.

On the PDP-11 mid-range processors the memory management unit is in the processor — so DMA transfers can only be to contiguous memory locations (ruling out the possibility of paging memory). The IBM Series 1 architecture (Figure 6.4) ensures all memory accesses are routed via the memory management unit.

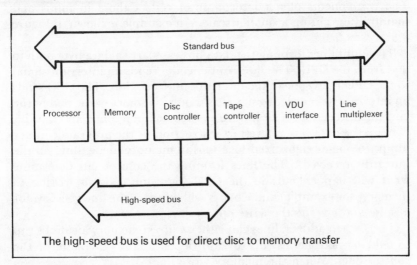

The high-speed bus is used for direct disc to memory transfer

Figure 6.3   Use of high speed bus on minicomputer

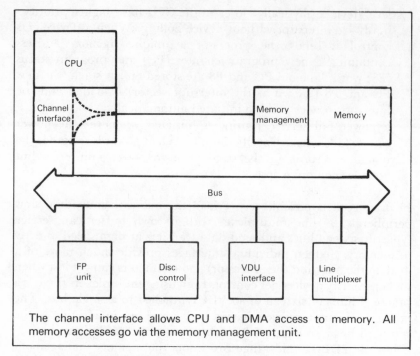

Figure 6.4   IBM Series 1 architecture

Microcomputer architecture

The components of a microcomputer reflect those in minis and mainframes, but on a smaller scale. An example is shown in Figure 6.5.

The eight lines forming the data bus can carry a data byte both to and from the CPU. The interrupt encoder sends an interrupt signal to the CPU if any one of the interrupt lines goes low. The CPU sends an interrupt acknowledge signal as soon as it comes to the end of the current instruction. The interrupt encoder then sends an eight-bit byte up the data bus as a restart instruction — the program counter jumps to one of eight fixed locations in memory (depending on the interrupt received). The lines forming the control bus determine what will happen outside the CPU (one line controls writing to memory, for example) and when it will happen (the line goes low for a pulse and *enables* the write operation).

The sixteen address lines can either address memory locations (up to 64k) or peripherals (up to 256) depending on the state of the *control* lines. When the memory write line MEMW goes low then the byte on the data bus (in the tristate buffer in fact) is written to

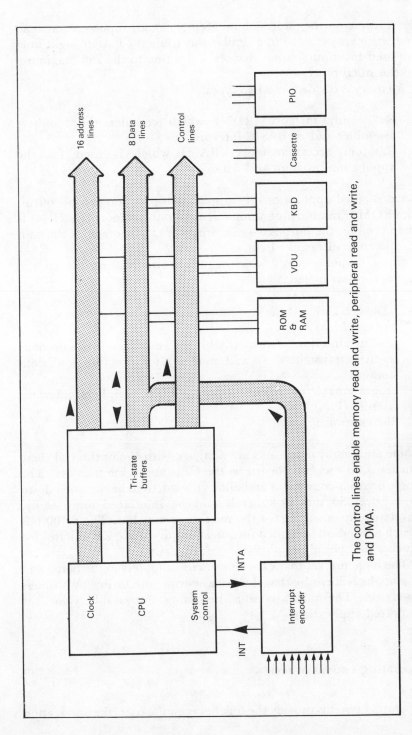

Figure 6.5   Microcomputer architecture (8-bit CPU)

the address on the address bus. Memory read, input/output read and write are actioned in a similar way (only the bottom eight lines are used for input/output devices — leading to the 256 maximum on this microprocessor).

Memory is divided into two types:

1. Read only memory (ROM) which contains the monitor, assembler and/or BASIC interpreter.
2. Random access memory (RAM) which is used for the application program and data.

For dedicated applications the application program can be 'burnt' into ROM. Erasable programmable read only memory (EPROM) is often used for the purpose — the program can be erased if the chip is exposed to ultraviolet light.

Input/output devices which can be attached readily to the microprocessor include:

— VDU (or TV);
— keyboard;
— cassette interface (with UART — universal asynchronous receiver/transmitter — and modem) for program and data storage;
— programmable input/output port (PIO) or peripheral interface adapter (PIA);
— disc controller.

Home and hobby computers are designed with two or three of these functions on the same board as the CPU and some memory. The single board is convenient and allows the micro to be designed down to a price. So that peripherals may be interfaced more easily, standards are emerging for the microprocessor bus. The S-100 bus is such a standard (designed for Intel 8080 and Zilog Z80 micros) for which a number of peripheral interfaces exist.

The huge market that exists for microcomputers in the home and as a hobby will ensure that the price continues to be low by business standards. The micro is thus becoming unbeatable value for dedicated applications.

Operating systems overview

Operating systems provide the link between the user, the application programs and the hardware. The main components can be divided into:

— user interface;
— device interface (and basic file accessing);
— memory and processor allocation;
— utility programs.

The concept is illustrated diagrammatically in Figure 6.6.

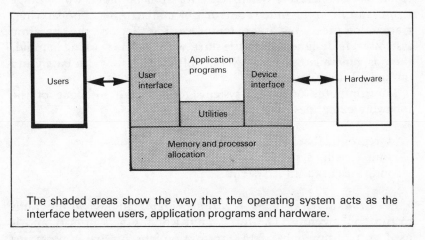

The shaded areas show the way that the operating system acts as the interface between users, application programs and hardware.

Figure 6.6   Operating system components

Mainframe operating systems

Mainframe operating systems were originally developed to optimise the processing of multiple batch streams. A teleprocessing system for example has to run as a job under the control of the operating system. This constraint leads to three main problems:

1. The additional layer of software means more software overhead (most large mainframes spend less than 50 per cent of their time in application programs — the rest of the time is spent on system overhead and scheduling).
2. Every additional type of on-line working (transaction processing, time-sharing, remote job entry) requires largely duplicated software which takes up substantial amounts of memory space — leaving as little as one-third of a one megabyte machine for application programs.

3. Terminal ports are dedicated to one type of working — or an additional layer of software is needed to provide application flexibilty.

We end up with a situation as in Figure 6.7 — complex and not very efficient.

Minicomputer operating systems

A number of operating systems exist for minicomputers which range from simple real-time control to concurrent time-sharing, transaction processing and batch processing. Because the operating systems were designed, from the start, with on-line working in mind, there is generally only one level of software — for both batch and on-line jobs (see Figure 6.8).

Minicomputer operating systems tend to fall into one of the following categories:

— foreground/background real-time systems;
— time-sharing systems;
— multi-user real-time systems.

Foreground/background real-time systems allow two programs to run concurrently. The foreground working gets priority and is used for real-time jobs, data transmission jobs and batch programs with low CPU requirements. Background working is suitable for on-line working, program development or an enquiry job.

Within a program it is possible to execute multiple tasks and thus to support several terminals. Tasks to be performed are linked in a simple chain according to their priority. The processor executes them one at a time starting with the task with the highest current priority.

All normal peripheral devices are supported including VDUs, floppy discs, discs, paper tape, magnetic tape, printers, cassettes and data transmission. Programming languages available normally include BASIC, interactive FORTRAN and assembler. The system is configured at run time and user program overlays are supported.

Time-sharing systems allow a number of different programs to get CPU attention on a round-robin basis. Runnable jobs are swapped between memory and disc to ensure that all jobs get into memory for some CPU attention. The operating system dynamically optimises the use of resources and it is possible to give specified jobs higher priority or longer time slices. In practice, good overall throughput is achieved by not allowing any one job to run continuously (time-

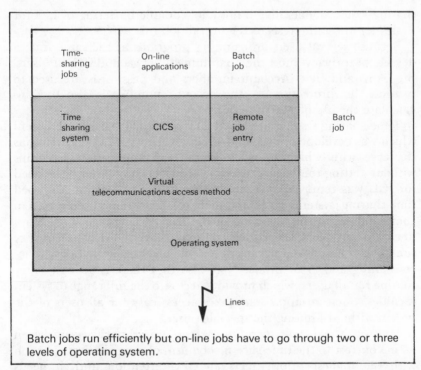

Batch jobs run efficiently but on-line jobs have to go through two or three levels of operating system.

Figure 6.7 Mainframe software overhead

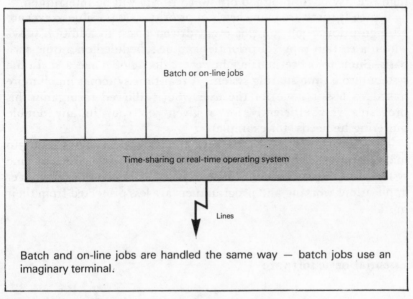

Batch and on-line jobs are handled the same way — batch jobs use an imaginary terminal.

Figure 6.8 Minicomputer operating system

sharing systems generally do not allow double buffering of I/O for example) in the interests of the overall job mix.

Because several users are running programs at the same time a degree of privacy must be maintained between different users' programs and files. Account numbers and passwords are used to provide this protection — the account number is also used to calculate the use of system resources.

Time-sharing systems are based on the original Dartmouth system which was developed in the mid-1960s. A feature of that system was the ease with which users could develop application programs without getting too bogged down in the operating system (the need for JCL was removed). Arguably the success of Dartmouth-based time-sharing systems owes as much to the common-sense system commands as to the invention of the BASIC language. Figure 6.9 illustrates a typical set of such commands. Without them (or very similar commands), program development becomes tedious, time-consuming and error prone. Note also that there is a single entry routine for all users, which provides access to the full range of system facilities. Such an approach makes access easy for all users of the system without limiting the specialist user.

Multi-user real-time operating systems are primarily event-driven — in contrast to the time-slice mechanism of time-sharing. The job with the highest priority gets all CPU attention until it needs input/output servicing or halts. If an event is declared of sufficiently high priority, a running job of lower priority will be interrupted.

Typically there are many levels of priority. It is possible to execute all high-priority jobs on this event-driven basis: in addition, tasks within a certain range of priorities can be scheduled on a time-slice basis. Such resource-sharing, however, does not make a real-time system into a time-sharing system. A real-time system is much more naked — less is done for the user who is allowed to organise his programs very efficiently for a given job (put in any double buffering he needs, for example).

The ease of use associated with time-sharing systems tends to make it most suitable for a commercial mix of jobs — the real-time system can be more efficient but it takes much longer to get applications working and programmers are less protected from their mistakes.

Essential basic software

Attractive hardware by itself is not enough. Remedying software

HELLO LOGIN LOGOUT BYE ATTACH	Commands exist to allow a user to 'sign on' to the system. Users give an account group code, individual code and password. The codes are used for both protection and accounting. This sign-on procedure is the only way into the system; once in, the user has access to the full range of system facilities (but not the files and programs of other users).
BASIC COBOL FORTRAN	Commands exist to identify the programming system being used.
NEW OLD APPEND RENAME SAVE RESAVE UNSAVE RESEQUENCE LIST DELETE RUN COMPILE	Commands exist to aid program development. The RUN command in particular is powerful: source statements are re-ordered, the source code is compiled, linked and executed. In addition to the commands, control characters are used to stop execution, stop/resume printing, suppress/enable printing, and delete character/line.
$EDIT $COPY $BACKUP $SPOOL $STATS	Utilities exist to aid file manipulation. These utility programs are in a system account which is available to all users on a 'use only' basis (only a privileged user can get at the programs to modify them).

Figure 6.9   Examples of system commands in a timesharing system

deficiencies delays system implementation and is very unproductive. While a degree of software development is probably always going to be necessary, there is a basic level below which the commercial user should not go.

The problem is not confined to small suppliers. The Level 6 machines from Honeywell and the Series 1 from IBM are both attractive machines — but they were announced with inadequate basic software (to the extent that they were unusable for a mix of on-line commercial jobs).

Here then is a checklist of essential basic software under the headings:

— operating system;
— basic utilities;
— file management.

Operating system

The worst situation to be in is to be developing application programs on an unfamiliar machine which has a new (and therefore untried) operating system. When things go wrong there is no stable base to start from. The error might be in the program, the operating system or the hardware and even a competent team will get demoralised quickly.

As a general rule, operating systems do not stabilise until their third release — which is typically two years after their first general release (not two years after their announcement). Do not suppose it will be different on the machine you are looking at — however attractive its other features. Once again the record of the big supplier is no better here than that of the smaller ones.

When selecting the proven operating system, first decide whether it is to be single-user or multi-user, foreground/background or multi-programming/time-sharing. Multi-tasking on a foreground/background system is not as secure as multi-programming or time-sharing. It is only really acceptable if the machine is to be dedicated to one application.

Other operating system requirements are:

— easy-to-use interface for program development (RSTS from DEC is good, for example, while RSX, also from DEC, is poor);
— support for high-level languages;
— accounts and passwords for sensitive applications;
— good file protection and lock-out mechanisms;
— facilities for sleeping programs and inter-program communications;
— adequate communications software.

At a simple level it must be possible to transmit files between two machines. If it is desired to have an interactive dialogue between machines, more facilities are needed. It is essential to split the communications function from the applications program in some way — perhaps using the interprogram communications features.

Basic utilities

A number of basic utilities are needed to assist program

development and to help the supervisor of a multi-user system. Programming aids include the compilers (assembly language and/or high-level language compilers/interpreters) and a simple editor (for amending program statements). Supervisor aids include a hardware error log, systems utilisation log (with appropriate analysis reports) and an on-line system status display.

File management

Efficient file management is an integral part of an on-line system. Access methods must include sequential file management (add records at the end, read the file sequentially) and direct access (block address relative to the start of the file). On all but the simplest systems some form of indexed access is also required. The indexed access method might be index sequential (ISAM), IAM or some form of sequential index — methods which were covered in Chapter 5.

In addition to the access method there need to be utilities to:

— create/delete files;
— copy files;
— dump/restore files;
— sort files;
— reorganise indexed files;
— spool print files.

It is not practical to dedicate the system printer on multi-user systems which is why some form of spooler is needed. Ideally it should be compact, simple to use and have the ability to call in 'line-up' and 're-run' routines.

Figure 6.10 summarises the essential basic software required. It may look a simple list but few minicomputers have been announced with even half of the items. It is all too easy to be dazzled by the hardware promise and to ignore software reality.

Choice of programming language

On minicomputers, as on mainframes, there is likely to be a choice of programming languages. Going from the low level to the high level, the choice is from:

— assembly language;

Proven operating system:	single-user or multi-user
	easy to use interface
	high-level languages
	adequate privacy
	file protection
	interprogram communications
	communication software
Basic utilities:	compilers
	editor
	hardware error analysis
	system utilisation analysis
	system status display
File management:	sequential and direct access
	indexed access
	indexed file reorganisation
	file create/delete
	file copy/dump/restore
	sort
	print spooler

Figure 6.10   Summary of essential basic software

— high-level language (e.g. BASIC, FORTRAN, COBOL);
— functional package (e.g. data entry, report generator, database management systems);
— application package (e.g. sales ledger, payroll).

Assembly language

As a general rule, assembly language should be avoided — unless the application is extremely time critical. It is true that assembly language is more efficient in its use of the computer (in the right hands), but it is difficult to get applications working quickly, it is difficult to document, it probably cannot be transported to another machine and, above all, it is difficult to maintain assembler programs.

An area where the use of assembler is justified is communications software — where the timing is very critical. In the past it has also been justified for a specific application which is to be repeated in many different locations — the pay-off coming from a smaller memory in every location. Such an approach, however, is getting increasingly difficult to justify — microcomputers can all have built-in BASIC; alternatively assembler can be compiled on a larger machine, and then burnt into read only memory (ROM), loaded from cassette or down-line loaded.

High-level language

When looking at high-level languages there have to be good reasons for not selecting COBOL or BASIC. FORTRAN, PL/1, ALGOL, PASCAL, CORAL, RTL2, APL all have their adherents but for a general mix of commercial applications COBOL and BASIC are *de facto* industry standards.

For batch applications on a mainframe, COBOL is always superior to BASIC. The language is standard, portable and relatively easy to read. For example:

PERFORM M600-PROCESS-MATCHED-GROUP.

is much easier to understand than:

GOSUB 6000

In addition, COBOL compilers have been optimised over a period of years to ensure high processing throughput (for example by generating efficient code and by double buffering input/output).

For on-line applications the choice between COBOL and BASIC is more difficult (assuming there is a choice). COBOL has the advantage, above, of being an industry standard which is portable and easy to read. It should not be supposed, however, that there is necessarily total portability between mainframe and mini, any more than between mainframe and mainframe. The ANSI 74 'standard' can be implemented at different levels for each of its modules — and usually is. Few minicomputer implementations, for example, include the SORT verb. Nevertheless portability can be achieved as long as a sensible subset of the language is used (and few of the '74 features).

The main query about the COBOL available will be its suitability for on-line applications. Is it supported by the transaction processing monitor? Can programs be compiled and executed at the same time? How easy is it to address the cursor and to format screens? Some implementations include ROW and COLUMN commands for cursor control as options in the DISPLAY and ACCEPT statements. It is also worth finding (or writing) a screen file maintenance suite to take the tedium out of screen formatting.

BASIC in its original Dartmouth form was not adequate for commercial applications (inadequate file handling and character manipulation). It has been extended, therefore, in a variety of (non-standard) ways. Other weaknesses include the slowness of the interpretive compiler in execution (efficient for complex instructions but not for simple ones) and the difficulty in reading the code. Its strengths include good interactive program development; it is quick to get applications up and the non-standard features allow:

— low-level instructions as well as high-level;
— good string handling;
— good file handling;
— screens designed in as the main input medium.

Functional and application packages

Functional packages are becoming available on minicomputers for a number of standard functions:

— data entry;
— database management;
— query languages;
— report generators.

These packages allow applications to be implemented more quickly at the expense of some machine efficiency. They are thus desirable aids for routine and low-volume applications, at least. They must, however, be integrated into the overall programming strategy. It is unlikely that a database management system will be efficient enough for a mainly transaction processing system (particularly on a mini). On the other hand a query language can be quite compatible with a conventional file structure.

The same considerations of consistency apply to the selection of application packages (covered further in Chapter 8). Application packages, unless entirely stand-alone, will use data entry, file management and print spooling methods which have to be consistent with others used in the installation. It follows that a careful examination of functional and application packages is an important early part of equipment selection.

Custom-built hardware

Although the aim should always be to use standard components, not every need can be satisfied this way. A degree of custom building may change an average solution into a very good one. The custom building might be a small (but essential) element of the whole project or it may require extensive development. To indicate the scope of what can be done, some examples are discussed under the headings:

— custom peripherals;
— operating environment improvements.

Custom-built software is covered in Chapter 8.

Custom peripherals

Because minicomputers have a relatively straightforward input/output interface, an industry has built up which can interface a variety of high-quality peripherals to the commonly available minicomputers. Standard peripherals like discs, tape drives and printers can be obtained from a specialist source (e.g. disc drives from CDC). Adding unusual peripherals (like a digitiser) which are not normally supported is also quite feasible. Often the peripheral can be attached through a VDU interface with no software modification, but if not the manufacturers will normally give advice on how to write input/output drivers and what hardware interface is required.

Sometimes these changes can be made to mainframes. One user who was unhappy with two-wire current loop-working persuaded his mainframe manufacturer to make a hardware modification which allowed four-wire working. Generally the current loop (20mA) interface is able to drive asynchronous terminals reliably at a greater distance than the EIA interface — particularly in buildings where the cable runs are likely to be in existing ducts (which are electrically very noisy). However, the EIA interface is required if modems are needed for remote working. It is possible to obtain 'level converters' which use LEDs and photoelectric cells to convert one to another and thus get the advantages of both solutions.

For remote asynchronous working, 300 baud is generally the maximum speed for two-way working (the 1200/75 baud modem is not generally suitable), but 'long-line drivers' are on the market which can be used instead of modems on leased lines. They are able to run at 2400 baud over distances of several miles. Running interactive VDUs at lower speeds than 2400 soon seems painfully slow to the operator, so the long-line drivers are a useful aid for remote working and perhaps standby.

Some operating systems support swapping discs in addition to data discs. Nowadays it is not a great deal more expensive to replace the swapping disc with bulk core memory. The bulk core appears to the operating system like the swapping disc and no software modification is necessary. Throughput is likely to be improved dramatically however.

Operating environment improvements

Many VDUs contain microprocessors which are programmed to carry out the VDU functions. The microprogram is either down-line loaded into random access memory (RAM) or it is stored in (replaceable) programmable read only memory (PROM). The same VDU can thus be given word-processing ability instead of or as well as data-processing ability. Designers can therefore get additional facilities built into the VDU to suit their application — rather than impose a heavy software load on the central machine.

It may also be appropriate to consider custom building the keyboard to suit the application. One bank has modified the numeric pad on its VDU keyboards to include '£', '$', 'M' and 'T'. The '£' and '$' are the most frequently used currencies; 'M' and 'T' represent Millions and Thousands, so reducing keying time and avoiding an opportunity for making errors. The keyboard also contains nine function keys — the key tops can be changed to suit the application. In their branch banking system the 'BGC' key generates a Bank Giro Credit entry for example. The use of function keys in this way again improves speed and reduces errors.

Generally the operator interface warrants close attention to avoid operator fatigue and ensure smooth and reliable operation. Voice response and voice recognition systems are available if the application needs them; the designer can also consider mark readers, badge readers, striped card readers and light pens.

System availability is an essential element of on-line systems. It means that there must be some fall-back arrangement if a major component fails. If a back-up system is installed it must be possible to switch VDUs and printers (for example) between systems. One way is to use a 'bus switch' but they are expensive. Another, simpler, approach is to have a patchboard built. Every VDU cable terminates in the patchboard with a conventional Din plug. The input lines to the computer have matching sockets so that it is an easy task to switch VDUs between the systems.

Similarly printer cables can terminate in plugs which can be moved between systems allowing either printer to be on either machine or both on one. So long as the operating system has been generated to expect two printers it will accept one or both being off-line.

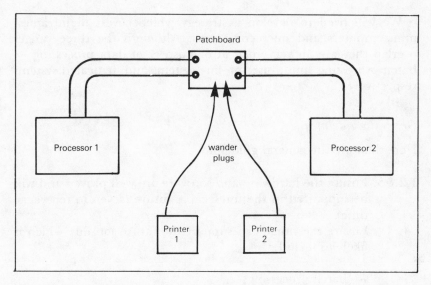

Figure 6.11 Switching printers between computers using plugs and sockets

A large number of devices are available which can significantly improve the way a system works. The ideas described are practical working examples of what can be done at low cost and low risk.

Choice of hardware

The ideal hardware would consist of a range of machines from micro through mini to mainframe, which are all programmed in the same high-level language, with proven hardware and comprehensive software, which can process efficiently a job mix of:

— batch programs;
— transaction processing;
— on-line program development;
— RJE, communications and message switching;
— time-sharing.

and which can run all existing applications.

No such perfect range exists — indeed perfection is often the enemy of the good. There will always be attractive new products announced, so the best we can do is to make sure the hardware strategy is right and that it is stable.

We will need to develop a strategy which covers mainframes, minicomputers and microcomputers. Although the three ranges overlap they are all very good at one aspect of data processing — batch processing, multi-user on-line systems and dedicated systems respectively.

General guidelines

Here then are the general guidelines:

1,2.&3. Ensure the hardware and software are well proven and will be supported in the foreseeable future (seven to ten years' time).

4. Ensure the range can support the future job mix which is likely to include:

    — batch processing;
    — transaction processing;
    — on-line program development;
    — RJE or other communications;
    — time-sharing.

5. Ensure the software includes the basic compilers and utilities described earlier in this chapter — for program development, file handling and system management.

6. Ensure there is a range of compatible machines available — a range that extends well above current plans.

7. Ensure that any initial machine is ordered well below the maximum configuration — after allowing capacity to process two heavy days in one (you wish to be able to recover from a day's hardware failure quickly).

8. Take account of the desirability of program portability — but note that batch programs are inherently different in structure from on-line transaction processing.

9. Take account of the problems of releasing new software on small machines. There must be some form of compatible media, down-line loading of programs or plug-in ROM.

10. Do not aim to use non-standard components as they will not be as reliable as standard products.

7 Workflow design

To the user, the most noticeable effect of distributed processing is the location of computer terminals at the work place — in the office and on the shop floor. But the designer is not just concerned with making the terminal convenient to use. He is concerned with the productivity of the whole business system — of which the terminal is just one component.

Even considering the VDU, let us be clear on our objectives before laying down guidelines. If the objective is to achieve the highest possible accurate throughput, different criteria will apply to an enquiry job and to a data entry application. For an enquiry job we want:

— ease of enquiry (using enquiry language, menu or function key);
— ease of reading significant results (using dual intensity, large characters or graphics, for example).

For a data entry job we want:

— ease of entry (enter fields in columns, 'protect' invalid screen areas, design keyboard for user application);
— ease of error correction (allow correction at character and field level, flash errors).

So we need to be clear on the main purpose of the application as we design the man-machine interface.

In this chapter we shall look at workflow design under the following headings:

1. Creating the right office environment;
2. Work posture and relaxation;
3. Flow of work;
4. VDUs and screen design;
5. Security of access and control;
6. Training and supervision;
7. Special purpose terminals.

Office environment

If people are to work well they must feel that they are doing a useful job and that their contribution is recognised. Working in a shabby office with poor ventilation and no proper temperature control is a signal that the management do not care about the staff — and the staff will respond accordingly. The minimum practical space requirement is sixty square feet (six square metres) per person. This figure includes an average allowance for corridors and access.

Comfortable working temperature is between 20°C and 25°C (68 to 77°F). Heating will be required in winter (which is effective from the start of work on Monday morning). Windows facing the sun should be screened to reduce summer heat and in hot climates air conditioning will be needed. Humidity should be maintained around 50 per cent — rather higher at cool temperatures (20°C) and a little lower at higher temperatures (25°C).

Ventilation should allow two to three air changes per hour. Ideally air extraction should be at floor level with air inlets under the windows or in the ceiling. If there are reasons for supposing that there is inadequate ventilation (stuffy atmosphere) trace gases can be introduced and the amount remaining measured at suitable intervals.

Carpets are preferable to tiles on the floor — in appearance, in acoustic properties and from ease of cleaning. The carpets should be treated with antistatic fluid and special carpets used near machinery.

Lighting is perhaps the most difficult area. Modern offices are frequently overlit because of the need to achieve a uniformity of lighting level (putting the ceiling fittings too far apart leaves dark areas in between). The current emphasis is to reduce the level of overall lighting (ambient lighting) and to supplement it with local lighting (task lighting). This approach puts the light where it is needed and tends to reduce overall energy costs. Here are some of the points to consider:

— use reflectors to push light out at 45° (less vertically down and less above 60° to the vertical) to avoid glare and to allow wider spacing of ceiling fittings;
— use cross louvres to prevent longitudinal glare from the lamps;
— aim for 800 lux per square foot (8000 lumens) overall;
— if a mixture of task and ambient lighting is used, ensure brightness is reasonably uniform so that staff will not have problems of adaptation as the eye moves from place to place.

Work posture

The human body is very adaptable but sitting or standing in uncomfortable positions soon leads to backache, muscle cramp or eyestrain. Sensible consideration for the needs of terminal operators will reduce fatigue and improve both throughput and accuracy.

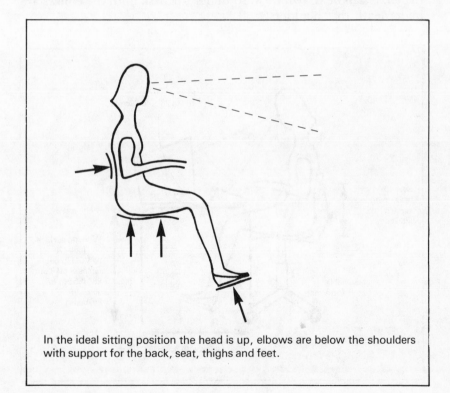

In the ideal sitting position the head is up, elbows are below the shoulders with support for the back, seat, thighs and feet.

Figure 7.1   Ideal sitting position

The principles of good seating are straightforward and illustrated in Figure 7.1. The body should be supported comfortably in the middle of the back, at the seat, across the thighs and at the feet.

As operators of many different sizes are expected to work at working surfaces of a fixed height, **it follows that adjustable chairs and footrests are essential.** Chairs set too low cause cramp across the shoulders (from hunching the back) and force too much weight on to the seat (rather than spread to the thighs). Lack of a footrest causes aches in the feet and knees of short people. The more the operator can work with her head up, the more comfortable she will be, as leaning forward stresses the lumbar region of the back.

If the documents are held on a document stand in front of the operator, with the keyboard central and the VDU to one side, then the head will be up (relaxing the spine) and there will be no need for the body to twist while looking at documents on the desk. Holding the hands too far forward also puts strain on the back muscles. **Chairs should not have arms** (or have them sufficiently low) so that the chair can be drawn forward under the desk until the elbows are underneath the shoulders.

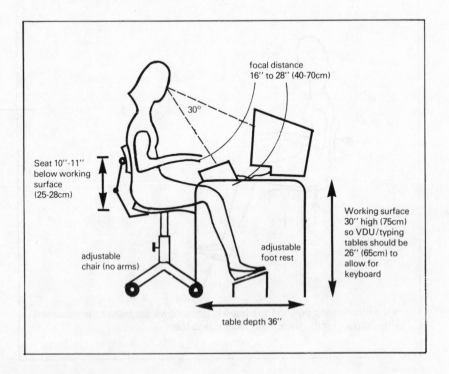

focal distance
16″ to 28″ (40-70cm)

30°

Seat 10″-11″
below working
surface
(25-28cm)

Working surface
30″ high (75cm)
so VDU/typing
tables should be
26″ (65cm) to
allow for
keyboard

adjustable
chair (no arms)

adjustable
foot rest

table depth 36″

Figure 7.2   Typical measurements

Typical working measurements

Figure 7.2 shows typical measurements for a VDU operator. The working surface should be consistently set at 75cm (30") so VDU and typing tables should be lower, 65cm (26"), to allow for the keyboard. The chair should be set 25 to 28cm (10" to 11") below the working surface and a footrest provided to support the feet. If the VDU is to be read more than 70cm (28") away — for example when the screen is to be shared for enquiries — use double width characters.

Eyestrain

Eyestrain can be caused by a number of factors and should be tackled promptly should it occur. The factors to consider are:

1. Is the lighting too strong or from the wrong direction causing glare? Lights should be above the VDU; the VDU should not be operated against the background of a window.
2. Characters on the screen should be easy to read with adjustable intensity. Generally the intensity should be turned down to the minimum level the operator is comfortable with.
3. Some operators have eye defects and should be wearing glasses — but vanity prevents them from doing so. The use of VDUs for any length of time will quickly expose such defects.
4. Strain may be caused by constantly changing eye focus — from screen to document to keyboard. This may be a training problem as experienced operators look less and less at the screen.
5. Operators should not spend more than two hours at a time on VDU intensive jobs. Carrying out a clerical job of which the VDU forms only a part provides a balanced mix of work which helps to avoid eyestrain.

Relaxation

The standard relaxation allowance for clerical work is fifteen per cent. In practice this allowance means six effective hours in a seven-hour working day. Note, however, that VDU operation tends to have a high degree of relaxation built in. The operator is usually not keying continuously but a screen at a time; the pause before the next screen contributes to relaxation. Nevertheless it is prudent to assume a six-hour working day for timing purposes.

Flow of work

Nobody likes to sit around waiting for work which arrives in a peak at the end of the day. It is up to the office manager to smooth the flow of work and to persuade other departments to push the work through regularly. The systems analyst also must be concerned with the smooth flow of work. Theoretical timing calculations tend to assume an even workflow which just will not happen unless it is designed in. Here are the main points to consider:

1. *Keep the movement of paper to a minimum.* Every handling operation requires a knowledge transfer, learning time and the possibility of delays. Minimising the paper movement therefore favours locating the VDUs on the clerical sections — rather than having a group of VDU operators.

    There are occasions when a group of specialist VDU operators is justified — normally in high volume, repetitive work, which is straightforward and which requires a very low knowledge transfer.

    Generally the VDU operation should be built into the work of the section — preferably operated by clerical staff as part of their job, or by specialists who are trained in the work of the section and can get any queries resolved on the spot.

2. *Aim to get a natural rhythm into the work.* It is not easy to build up speed if every job is different from the one before. The work goes faster and there are fewer errors if, for example, like jobs are grouped together, if different types of work are done on different sections, if clerical staff get used to dealing with their own customers. VDU screens and input programs can be designed to take advantage of the need for rhythm in the clerical work: assume the same type of transaction will be repeated, for example, rather than always going back to the menu.

3. *Design out the peaks and troughs.* Every job has its peaks and troughs. They are the most vulnerable part of any job and the temptation is to ignore them and hope they will go away. Distributed computing provides a real opportunity for removing peaks — by anticipating them or mechanising them. Identify first the daily, weekly and monthly peaks in the system under review — but also the preceding operations and the following operations. Look for ways of smoothing peaks in all stages of the process. For example: use exception reports to warn of likely problems the day before they are due, mechanise the sending of telex messages, post payments expected automatically so that

input is reduced to the ones that are wrong, optimise input programs which are required at peak input times to improve throughput, provide enquiry facilities and reference reports so that queries can be resolved quickly.

4. *Avoid overmanning with staff flexibility.* A weakness of the section approach (autonomous working group) is that the section leader is inclined to staff for his peaks. If there are many small sections, all staffed for peaks, there will be considerable overmanning in the department as a whole. The problem can be avoided in some or all of the following ways: sections should not be too small (ten is a good working size), staff should be cross-trained systematically within the section and across sections, extra VDUs should be available for sections to use at peak times, mechanisms should exist for staffing heavily loaded sections from those which are more lightly loaded (with an informal review every so often). It is instructive to note that good supermarkets plan the deployment of staff (at checkout, stores, stock control, resting) in quarter hour slots with continuous monitoring.

Concentrating on these points will help the systems analyst to work with the clerical staff management to achieve an even flow of work which is both interesting and seen to be fair.

VDUs and screen design

VDUs available on the market range from simple teletype compatible machines to sophisticated models under microcomputer control. The simple models rely on the host computer for intelligence and send characters up the line as they are keyed. The more advanced models can send data to the host a field at a time or a screen at a time. They can also carry out a degree of error checking (which is generally limited to field size checks — characters cannot be keyed into 'protected' positions).

The choice of machine depends on the application, but it is desirable to have consistency of VDUs across applications. The operating system will only be able to recognise a limited number of control codes, it is easier for operators to get familiarity with one type of terminal and standby is also simpler with a single type.

Function keys are a useful way of tailoring the VDU to an application while keeping to a standard model. The keytops can be changed to suit the application (use sticky labels in an emergency).

Hitting a function key does not affect the display but can cause a control sequence (e.g. ESC followed by P) to be sent to the host computer. The programmer can use this sequence to indicate a transaction type (instead of a menu) or to generate standard narrative.

VDU manufacturers will allow users to specify their own codes to suit their application. Figure 7.3 gives an example of the options on powering up the VDU and Figure 7.4 gives a summary of the control codes for one user-specified VDU.

Example of options on powering up

When the terminal is powered up or the INIT key is pressed, the screen is cleared, a single character is accepted from the keyboard to indicate transmission speed as follows:

Speed (baud)	Full duplex	Half duplex
	key response	
300	E	U
600	F	V
1200	H	X
2400	J	Z
4800	L	
9600	N	

The terminal then assumes the following status:

Keyboard	*enabled* (can be disabled to the operator, during printing from the screen, for example)
Block mode	*off* (transmission is character by character)
Format mode	*off* (screen positions can be set 'protected' or 'unprotected'. Where format mode is 'on', the VDU only processes unprotected fields)
Double size	*off* (characters can be displayed double size)
Line drawing	*off* (special codes are used for line drawing)
Protection flag	*off*
Video mode	*normal* (can be half intensity, blink or underline)
Protected video mode	*half intensity* (mode for protected fields)
Insert character	*off* (character can be inserted in a line)
Bits/character	*7+ parity*
Parity	*even*
Stop bits	*1*
Full/half/duplex	*Key response* ⎫
Transmit and receive speed	*key response* ⎬ see key response above

---

Figure 7.3 Example of VDU features

The ASCII character set is illustrated in Figure 4.5. An example of the use of control codes is shown below:

Code	Hex	Effect	Code	Hex	Effect
BEL	07	Audible alarm	DC1	11	Resume sending
BS	08	Back space	DC3	13	Stall sending
HT	09	Tab (to next un-protected field)	ESC	1B	Special sequence follows (see below)
LF	0A	Line feed	FS	1C	Start protected field
VT	0B	Back tab (to start of previous unprotected field)	GS	1D	End protected field
				20-7E	Displayable characters
FF	0C	Clear screen			
CR	0D	Carriage return ('send')	DEL	7F	Rubout (ignored)
SO	0E	Enter graphics mode			
SI	0F	Exit graphics mode			

Escape (1B)

followed by:	Causes	followed by:	Causes
A	Cursor up	P	Delete character
B	Cursor down	Q	Enter insert character mode
C	Cursor right		
D	Cursor left	R	Exit insert character mode
H	Home cursor		
I	Clear screen	T	Enable keyboard
J	*Clear to end screen	U	Disable keyboard
K	*Clear to end line	W	Write nulls
*In format mode, only unprotected fields are cleared		X	Send
		Y	Position cursor
L	Start double width	Z	Sense cursor
M	Enter format mode	[	End protected field
N	Exit format mode	]	Start protected field
O	Print screen contents at 300 baud	^	+ Set protected video mode
		←	+ Set video mode

+ video modes include half intensity, blink and underline

Function keys on the keyboard have no effect on the display. Keys 1 to 9 generate ESC followed by p to x.

Figure 7.4 Example of control codes

Screen design

There are certain general guidelines to follow in the design of
screens:

1. *Make the screen easy to use.* Organise the screens to follow the
   logical flow of the problem but do not break them up
   artificially. The pause between screens breaks up the operator's
   rhythm and slows down input. If the question-and-answer type
   of dialogue is used, line up answers in one column and justify
   the questions to the right. Display computer-generated replies to
   the right of, or below, the answer; not below the question. For
   example:

   CUSTOMER CODE: **HILLSAM**
   BRANCH: **EC2P**
                   HILL SAMUEL & CO LIMITED
                   45 BEECH STREET
                   LONDON EC2P 2LX

   If formatted screens are used, design the screen to look like the
   source document (but do go back to the source, not an
   intermediate document created for the computer).
       Make sure the entries are in a logical and natural sequence
   which the operator will find easy to follow. Make sure the style of
   the screens is consistent throughout the project.
2. *Provide a consistent response to questions.* Nothing is more
   irritating to an operator than having to use different default
   responses. If it is left to the individual programmer (or even the
   individual analyst) differences are bound to emerge. Standard
   responses include:

none	standard default entry
END	end of input
DDMMYY	date (displayed as DD-MMM-YY)
X	exit this screen
N,C,D,Q	new, change, delete, enquire
Y,N	yes, no
↑	retains last value of this field

   With question and answer, error messages are displayed and the
   prompt repeated. Using formatted screens, errors are flashed
   and the bottom line of the screen is reserved for error messages.

3. *Minimise the need for reference to manuals.* Operator manuals should be used mainly for reference, not during routine running. So make the questions meaningful and show possible answers. A prompt of:

CONFIRM (Y OR N)?

is clear and easy to understand. On formatted screens possible replies can be listed to the right of the unprotected answer field. Consider building in a HELP response if there are many possible replies.

4. *Minimise the operator's keystrokes.* Where possible, the operator should enter nothing (if the answer can be assumed, for example the date) or the first letter of a sensible reply. M, F indicate Male and Female more clearly and more reliably than 1 and 2. During file maintenance, display all fields if a new record is to be added to the file. Otherwise, existing entries are displayed and fields changed by number (question and answer) or in place (formatted screen). D deletes the record, X merely exits.

Data entry screen design

Minicomputers allow two modes of data entry. In question and answer mode (as in Figure 7.5) the prompting questions come one line at a time. The answer is accepted and validated and the next prompt sent to the screen. Using formatted screens (as in Figure 7.6) the screen is designed to look like the source document and the operator 'fills in the blanks'. Both modes have their advantages.

Question and answer allows validation during input and the pattern of questions can be varied depending on the answers received. There is also no limit to the depth of the form — the screen is rolled up as every line is entered. Formatted screens impose less overall load on the processor (one processing burst per screen rather than processing one field at a time). Their rigidity also has merit in that the operator can build up speed on a fixed pattern of input. They are also the only realistic way of working to a mainframe (because of the penalties of servicing the screen one field at a time).

Figure 7.5 illustrates the way a question and answer type dialogue might proceed. The example is taken from an order-processing application and illustrates the entry of order header information. Notice that the prompting questions have been right-justified and the answers left-justified. The purpose is to help the operator distinguish the prompts from the replies. Note also that after the

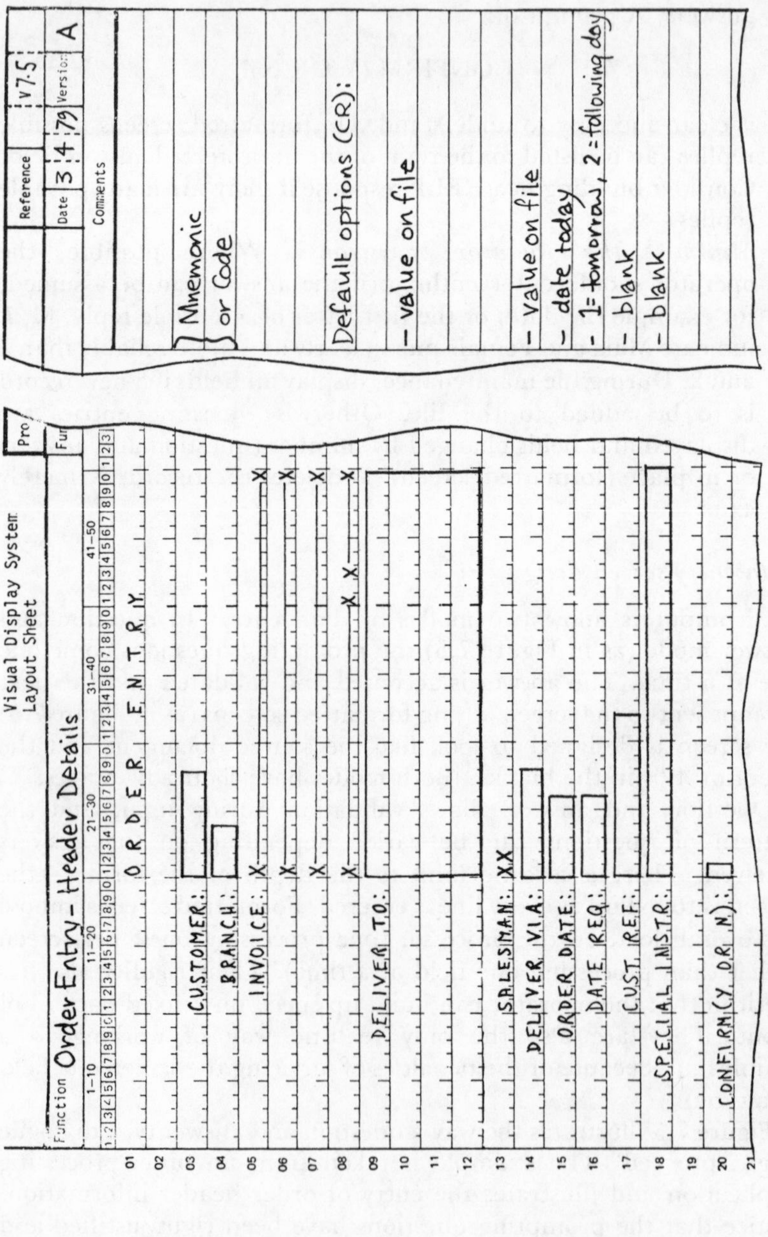

Figure 7.5 Example of screen using question and answer mode

customer and branch have been identified (by code or mnemonic), the remaining fields have 'default' options. The normal delivery address is held on file — hitting *carriage return* (CR) causes the standard delivery address to be displayed — alternatively the operator can over-ride the computer and enter a special delivery address. Only the invoice address and salesman code cannot be over-ridden in this way.

Here then are the general rules to observe if high throughput is to be achieved:

— Organise the screen entries in the same sequence as the originating document (it is very difficult for operators if they have to pick out fields randomly). If there is no source document (telephone orders for example), organise the entries into a logical sequence which helps the operator (to prompt all order details) — consider redesigning the source document if it is not logical.
— Design data entry for speed and accuracy. Build the most common replies into the computer as default options. For example, try to avoid entering dates — store the next five working days and allow the operator to respond with:

   CR   today's date;
   1   next working day;
   2   following working day, etc.

— Program to minimise errors. Carry out validation and consistency checks and query unlikely replies. As the reply is often a meaningful alphabetical letter, hold this character in the program as a literal rather than translating it into a number (for GOTO...DEPENDING ON...). The program is easier to understand and maintain if the literals are held in clear.

Figure 7.6 illustrates the same problem as shown in Figure 7.5 but using a formatted screen. The screen has been designed to look like the printed order confirmation. Unlike question and answer the computer generated replies (invoice address, salesman and the default values) do not appear until the whole screen has been sent. An alternative input method therefore is to tabulate the questions first:

   CUSTOMER:
     BRANCH:
   DELIVER TO:
       etc.

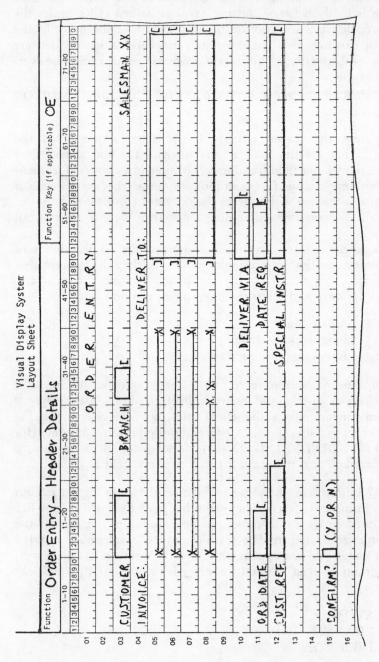

Figure 7.6 Example of formatted screen

and then to display the formatted results. This second approach is better when there are relatively few entries to be made into a complicated screen.

Figure 7.7 illustrates the way to design an input screen where the data is repetitive. The use of column headings allows more to be entered on each screen while keeping the screen easy to understand and use. In this example the product code and quantity fields are close together as they are entered at the same time. At convenient intervals the operator should send the screen for validation (formatted input) and confirm the entries so far (question and answer).

For data entry applications calculate VDU time as follows:

	Keystrokes per hour
Highly interactive (question and answer)	5500
Moderately interactive (entering descriptive data)	7200
Formatted screen	10 sec per screen + 9000

Enquiry screen design

When designing a system for enquiries the systems analyst's main concern is to make the system easy to use. It is always possible to learn how to use even a complicated system — provided it is used constantly. It is altogether more difficult to make an infrequently used system easy. Enquiry programs fall into three categories:

— *Special purpose programs* which are designed to answer a fixed pattern of enquiries efficiently (e.g. what are the orders outstanding for customer ABC?).
— *Report generators* which extract records (with selection), sort them into a specified order and print the results (with control breaks and totalling). The criteria for selection, sorting, printing and totals are determined by using field names and logical operators e.g.:

SELECT IF	DOB ≤ 101231
SORT ON	GRADE — SUBTOTAL
WITHIN	TYPE — PAGE TOTAL
PRINT	TYPE
	GRADE
	NAME
	DOB
	SALARY

Report generators of this type are suitable for quick one-off reports where the print format is not too critical (the report generator formats the output into columns automatically).

— *Tree search routines* along the lines of the Prestel service provided by the British Post Office. The method is illustrated in Figures 7.8 to 7.11. Fintel is an information provider which is owned jointly by the Financial Times and Extel. The Fintel front page (Figure 7.8) is obtained by keying '*248#' into the Prestel connected television set. If it is desired to read the American News, the response will be '0' which gives page 24800 (Figure 7.9). Responding '2' now gives page 248010 (Figure 7.10) and responding '2' again gives page 5310102 (Figure 7.11) — the one desired. If this page is likely to be used frequently it would be quicker to make a note of the page number and next time to key '*5310102#' at the beginning. Prestel thus caters for both experienced and inexperienced enquirers.

Additional features in Prestel which show attention to enquiry needs include:

* * #   go back to the frame I saw last (up to three times);
* * *   cancel the entries I have just been making;
* *00 repeat the frame which has been displayed (if there is noise on the line for example);
* *09 repeat the frame which has been displayed with any updates which may have just occurred;
* *3 # show local information index page.

Security of access

The account identification and password mechanism provided by DEC with their RSTS operating system is a useful standard for

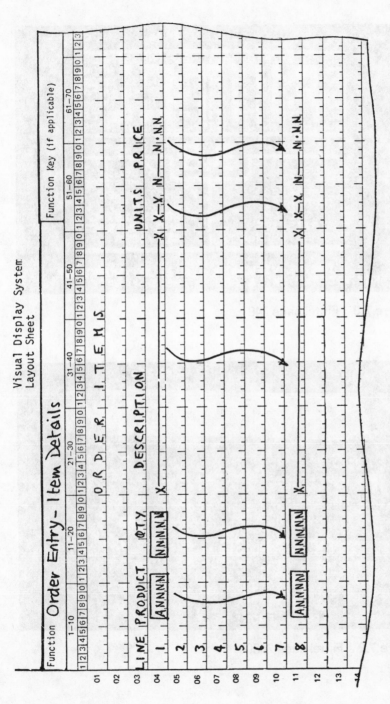

Figure 7.7   Example of tabulated entries

Figure 7.8   Fintel page 248

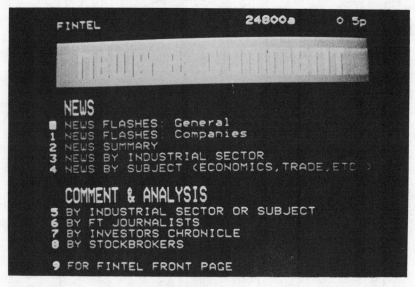

Figure 7.9   Fintel page 24800

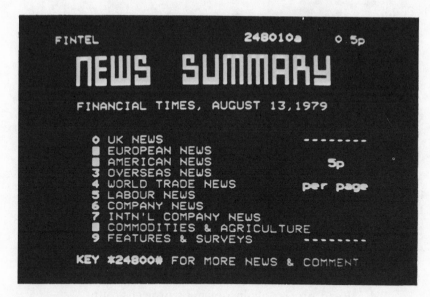

Figure 7.10 Fintel page 248010

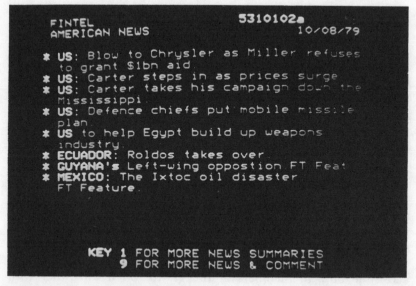

Figure 7.11 Fintel page 5310102

assessing security of access. There are three components in the signing on procedure:

— project group number;
— owner number (for each individual);
— owner's password.

So the sequence:

£18,11
Password: CELESTE

indicates project group 18 with owner 11 whose password is *CELESTE* (which in fact does not get displayed on the VDU as it is keyed).

With every file (data or program) is associated a protection code:

1	Read protect against owner;
2	Write protect against owner;
4	Read protect against owner's project group;
8	Write protect against owner's project group;
16	Read protect against other groups;
32	Write protect against other groups;
64	Executable program; can be run only;
128	Special privileges apply.

These codes can be used in combination. For example, the default protection for a compiled BASIC Plus program is 124 (64 + 32 + 16 + 8 + 4) denying access to all but the owner.

Project group 1 is used by the system manager and is known as the privileged account. Privileged account users can access any file in any other account. The account also contains the library of installation utilities. A filename preceded by '$' causes the system to look in the library in account [1,2]. For example, in the statement:

RUN $HSEDIT

the program HSEDIT is found in account [1,2]. Similarly the prefix ! means [1,3], % means [1,4], and & means [1,5]. The prefix # has a special meaning. It indicates owner '0' in the current project group. This feature allows a project group library to be created which is accessible only to members of the group. So if an owner with account [18,11] issues the instruction:

APPEND # ISAM

the ISAM routines would be found in account [18,0].

This two-level account structure with passwords and protection codes allows as much protection as is likely to be necessary. Programs and files can be made available at the individual, project group and system level.

Restricted access

Generally there should be restricted access to mainframe and minicomputers to reduce the risk of:

— accidental damage;
— vandalism;
— theft of media and components;
— environmental change;
— noise.

A half-glazed partitioning wall with a magnetic card lock on the door is straightforward to install and restricts access adequately for most purposes.

If the central printers are used with a need for regular distribution of output, it may be more convenient for them to be in their own room. It will be easier to service the printers without having people tramping in and out of the main computer room. Printers create the most dust and noise of all the peripherals — another reason for separating them.

Access at the keyboard level can be restricted by the use of keyboard locks. Generally the account and password system gives adequate protection but keyboard locks are necessary if the VDU is located in a public place.

Training and supervision

The distributed system is to be run by the user managers, section leaders and staff. If they are to use it successfully all the rules of good management apply:

— staff need to understand the job they are doing, not just follow a set of rules mechanically;
— staff need to know where the job fits into the organisation and that it is a useful job;
— staff need to be trained in how to do the job; they may need both business training and skills training (e.g. keyboard);

— staff need to be successful at the job they are doing; failure leads to dissatisfaction and a tendency to cover up any problems;
— staff need their contribution to be recognised, in terms primarily of esteem but also in adequate remuneration levels;
— staff need extra help, at a time of change, in the control and reconciliation areas particularly.

Notice that training in the use of the VDUs for a specific application is only on the list indirectly. This is the area that computer training often concentrates on, but VDUs in general make systems easier to use, not more difficult.

A particular problem arises during the introduction of a new system, for systems are most vulnerable at a time of change. Familiar rules are no longer the help they used to be and it is not easy to see what is important and what is not — unless there is real understanding of the business and the new solution. The systems analyst can help the user managers most if he:

— has in-depth understanding of the business;
— has simulated all aspects of the new system before going live;
— has a plan for gradual take-on;
— has built in comprehensive processing controls so that mistakes can be detected and rectified quickly.

The user executive responsible for implementation has an even more important role. He has to ensure:

— his organisation structure is right for the new system;
— he has the right calibre of manager and section leader (a sloppy system now is a warning signal);
— the staff are cross-trained in advance of any changes;
— the gradual take-on and controls are built into the plan (as above);
— errors and backlogs of work are investigated and actioned at once.

Special purpose terminals

So far in this chapter it has been assumed that the VDU is the main type of distributed terminal. While the VDU is versatile and suited to office work, purpose-built terminals in a given situation can:

— achieve higher throughput with accuracy;
— satisfy a broader need;
— reduce cost to acceptable levels.

Higher throughput with accuracy can be achieved with devices that reduce the need for keying. Examples include:

— badge readers on the shop floor or in security systems where a job or an individual needs to be identified;
— point of sale terminals which identify products which have been pattern encoded;
— voice recognition systems, the next major area for technical advance.

Broader needs can be satisfied by dual purpose terminals. Examples include:

— cash dispensers which identify the user before servicing the request;
— pocket data capture devices for roundsmen and meter readers — data is captured and any reconciliation carried out without further transcription.

Cost reduction can be achieved by taking advantage of widely used domestic appliances. Examples include:

— domestic television sets linked to Viewdata services;
— touch-tone telephones which can be used for keying numeric data (including codes) with a confirming voice response.

With wide availability of microprocessors it is possible to think of ways of making terminals 'smart'. Giving the terminal intelligence can make the user interface simpler, reduce errors and provide the opportunity for earlier error detection and correction.

Summary

Not all the points covered in this chapter are under the control of the systems analyst — or even of the user manager. But it can be seen that there is more to workflow design than just screen layouts. No one factor will cause problems but in combination the wrong environment can destroy attempts to introduce efficient systems.

Make sure that the major obstacles to efficiency are removed:

— the right office environment and lighting;
— the right office furniture and work posture;
— a smooth flow of work avoiding peaks and troughs;
— sensible design of VDU and screen;
— adequate staff and supervisor training;
— the use of special-purpose terminals to satisfy particular requirements.

8 Deciding the programming strategy

Installing a distributed system is likely to involve new hardware and unfamiliar software. The trap to avoid is allowing application program development to start in earnest before the computer system is understood fully. First, the software tools should be developed and refined on pilot programs.

If the application programmers start too early, they will inevitably have to rework parts of their programs as they experience the waste associated with 'all learning together'. The purpose of this chapter is to highlight the difference between application programming and the development of software tools. It is also the intention to show that application program development is more reliable if a standard and proven approach is adopted. The chapter covers:

— design principles for on-line programs;
— examples of program suites;
— building the software functions;
— using standard packages.

On-line program design

On-line systems can reduce errors and complexity by validating the data entered *in context*. Customer orders can be checked against stock levels before the order is accepted; the customer's name and address can be checked against the order to make sure we have the right one; cash can be allocated to invoices and the customer's credit balance updated. So on-line input is more than just data entry. To get the real benefits, main files must be on-line to the data entry programs and in many cases they will be updated in real time. Here then are the requirements of an on-line system:

1. Data should be validated in context.
2. All input should be proof listed in some way — journal entries would be listed, customer orders would be on an order confirmation, a name and address change would be on a change report.
3. Recovery from failure should be included in the design — the need for re-keying should be avoided by logging the input and letting the computer reprocess the work after a failure.
4. On multiple VDU systems a common printer cannot, in practice, be run by the data entry programs.

Given these requirements, there are three ways of carrying out the functions of data entry (DE), updating (UPD) and reporting (RP). The three ways can be described as follows:

1. *Real-time updating.* The real-time updating approach is illustrated in Figure 8.1. This approach is well suited to main file maintenance because there are relatively few file insertions and there is a need for the file to be kept constantly up to date. If transaction data is to be validated in context it must be possible to correct errors or to make changes to static data with immediate effect. If a new customer is to be processed the sooner he is on the file the better. If an address or credit limit is wrong, it needs to be put right.

   Using this approach for maintaining a master file, the data entry program lets the operator verify the data entered before updating the master file. It then writes a second copy of the updated record (called an 'after image') to the change file. The change file can be used for fast recovery (the records are dated and timed to assist recovery) as well as for the change report. In this example the change report might well consist of record sheets to be filed for reference purposes (the new sheet would replace the old in the filing cabinet).

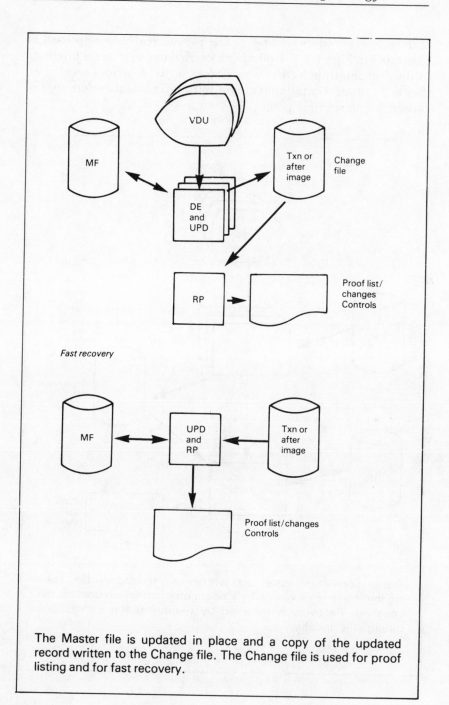

The Master file is updated in place and a copy of the updated record written to the Change file. The Change file is used for proof listing and for fast recovery.

Figure 8.1   Real-time updating

2. *Pseudo real-time updating.*   The pseudo real-time approach is illustrated in Figure 8.2. Updating is carried out by a single program (instead of multiple VDUs) which picks up transactions soon after they are written. Updating is almost instantaneous, therefore, but is carried out at a single point.

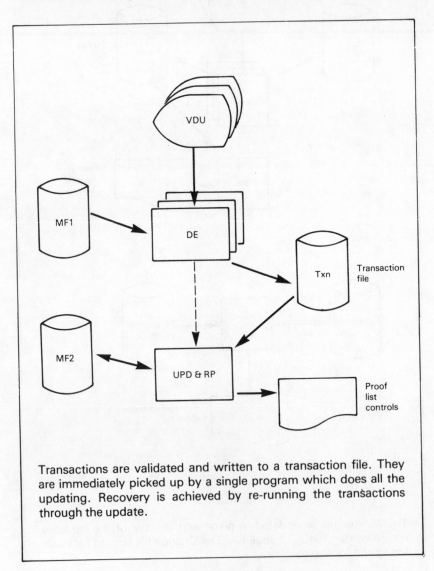

Transactions are validated and written to a transaction file. They are immediately picked up by a single program which does all the updating. Recovery is achieved by re-running the transactions through the update.

Figure 8.2   Pseudo real-time updating

The purpose of this approach is to reduce potential queuing problems in the data entry programs and to split out work that can sensibly be delayed a few seconds. It applies in situations such as foreign exchange dealing where currency positions and limits need to be updated from transactions — but the positions and limits files are not needed during data entry. The data entry programs are thus kept smaller and a potential bottleneck is removed. It also makes recovery after a failure easier in an order-processing system (if recovery is more important than the update delay).

3. *On-line input with batch updating.* On-line input with batch updating is illustrated in Figure 8.3. This approach recognises the problems associated with adding new transaction records to a file. It aims at combining the virtues of validation in context (an account balance field on the master file record is updated by the transaction) with secure file updating (the transaction history file is updated on a father-son basis) and control (the account balance in the master record is checked against the total of the transaction records). The approach is well suited to applications such as sales ledger, purchase ledger and payroll where a transaction file is maintained in addition to the master file.

In practice an on-line system will use a combination of these three approaches depending on the requirements of the individual procedures.

Examples of program suites

A common error is to underestimate the number of programs that there will be in the final system (could you write down all the programs in a payroll or purchase ledger system before reading on?). And yet the program suites tend to fall into a number of standard patterns. If we consider systems such as sales ledger, payroll, purchase ledger there will be:

— one or more master files (customer, employee, supplier);
— one or more transaction files (sales ledger, payroll variable data, purchase ledger).

The program suites (procedures) fall into these patterns:

— master file maintenance, enquiry, security, recovery (along the lines of Figure 8.1);

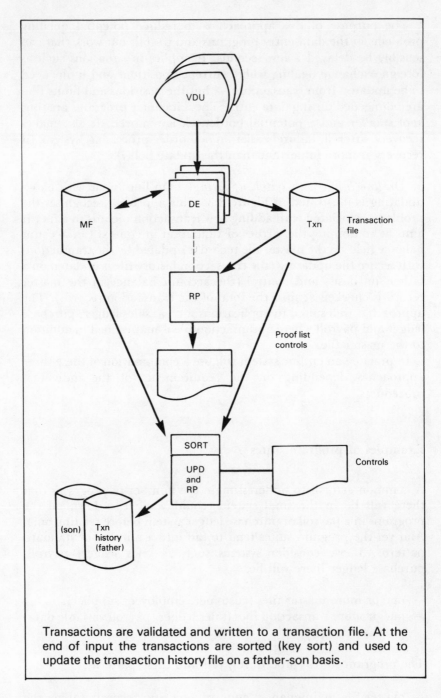

Transactions are validated and written to a transaction file. At the end of input the transactions are sorted (key sort) and used to update the transaction history file on a father-son basis.

Figure 8.3   On-line input — batch update

— transaction input, control, file update, security, recovery (along the lines of Figure 8.3);
— mainstream processing and reporting;
— periodic transaction file clear down;
— conversion suite from old system to new.

To illustrate this checklist, the following are typical programs in a standard payroll system and a purchase ledger system.

Payroll system

The payroll is based on three master files (employee, bank, tax tables) and a transaction file (employee variable data).
Master file maintenance:

— Employee file   insert, change, delete, enquire
                        changes list
                        full list
                        fast recovery
                        reorganise
— Bank file   insert, change, delete, enquire
                        changes list
                        full list
                        reorganise
— Tax tables   insert, change, delete, enquire
                        changes list
                        full list

Transaction processing:

— Employee variable data   input
                                    proof list
                                    sort
                                    update
                                    full list by name or cost centre
                                    enquire

Mainstream processing:

— Payroll   build up to gross
                     gross to net
— Print   pay advice
                     payroll journal
                     pay cheque

> credit transfer
> transfer journal
> cash analysis by pay station
> list by cost centre

Periodic purge:

— Clear down   transactions

File conversion:

— File   read
>   sort
>   build

A total of twenty-nine programs (excluding back-up, restore, sort and copy programs).

Purchase ledger system

The purchase ledger is based on a single master file (supplier) and two transaction files (purchase ledger and purchase analysis). The purchase ledger file contains what is owed to the supplier; the purchase analysis file contains an analysis for internal accounting.

Master file maintenance:
— Supplier file   insert, change, delete, enquire
>   changes list
>   full list
>   fast recovery
>   reorganise

Transaction processing:

— Invoice, credit note input
— Journals, urgent invoice input
— Transactions   proof list
>   sort
>   ledger file update
>   sort
>   analysis file update
>   ledger file list/enquire
>   analysis file list/enquire

Mainstream processing:

— Payments   due report, cash flow
              selection
              proof list
— Print   remittance advices
              cheques
              traders' credits
              payment summary
              overdue list, controls
— Update   ledger file with payments

Periodic purge:

— Post nominal ledger
— Clear down transactions

File conversion:

— File   read
          sort
          build

A total of twenty-five programs (excluding back-up, restore, sort and copy programs).

It is not surprising that subsystems of this type take 400 to 500 man days to design, specify, program, test and implement. Looking at the job in this systematic way helps to ensure that nothing gets forgotten — it also helps to show that the same types of program are used repetitively, and that a set of proven standard functions/utilities will make the job go much faster.

Building the software functions

Figure 8.4 contains a checklist which summarises areas where common functions may be necessary. The 'strategic programmer' on the project has the job of identifying the technical needs, seeing what is available and remedying any deficiencies.

1. *File handling:* file and record descriptions, special file access routines, logical file dumps, use of parameter files for batch/generation control, common tables.

2. *Field handling:* field validation, packing/unpacking (name and address, arithmetic fields), date conversion, days between dates, output field editing, complex functions.

3. *Peripheral handling:* VDU characteristics, cursor control, page mode, screen formats, conventions for operator response, handling special peripherals.

4. *System utilities:* start up, close down, back-up, restart/recovery, usage statistics, sort, spooler, transaction file handler.

5. *Purchased and supplied software:* TP monitor, operating system, account numbers and passwords, system housekeeping, communications protocols, report generators.

6. *Programming conventions:* standards for documentation, structure, layout, prohibitions, efficiency guides, standard program skeletons for match/merge, analysis, page printing, vets.

Figure 8.4   Checklist of software functions

The points in figure 8.4 are expanded below:

1. *File handling.*   File descriptions with field names should be set up for common use. Special access routines need to be identified and any deficiencies or omissions remedied. The task includes examining unfamiliar software for problem areas or inefficiency. It may be necessary to write the access routines and as a guide a first-class systems programmer will take about 100 man days to write an ISAM routine, assuming he already understands the technique well.

   Parameter files are used to control file generations, run dates, batch numbering and to contain common tables. The file will be used by many programs and should be set up in advance. Logical file dump programs should be written for all files to simplify system testing.

2. *Field handling.* Field validation subroutines should be prepared. Examples of field validation include numeric field, check digit verification, valid date, range check and also standard error messages. Field packing subroutines which may be needed include name and address, date, large numbers and conversion of arithmetic fields to different representations.

Dates always require special routines as they are required in a variety of formats, e.g. 31.10.78, 10.31.78 (USA), 31-OCT-78, 781031 (for sorting) or 3226 (days since 1 January 1970). It may also be necessary to calculate the days between two dates, and to verify the 'next working day'.

Field editing is required for the output and display of numbers (with and without leading zeros), codes (insertion of hyphens to show structure), floating asterisk (or £ or $) and representation of amounts in words.

Complex arithmetic or logical functions may need to be given special treatment: calculation of gross redemption yield, discounted cash flow calculations, leasing calculations ·— requiring expert knowledge which is unlikely to be in the project team.

3. *Peripheral handling.*   VDU handling utilities include terminal characteristics, cursor control, page mode working, screen format utilities, retrieval methods and transmission techniques. Conventions for operator response must be uniform across programs and systems — so that VDU operators in particular are not confused when they change applications. Standard responses were illustrated on p.138.

Most new systems will require peripherals which are new to the project team. Special handling routines may be required for these devices as well as for those which are being used in an unfamiliar way.

4. *System utilities.*   System utilities are required for start of day to set the date and time and to initialise background and sleeping programs. Similarly utilities are needed for end-of-day closedown, file back-up and security, restart and recovery and system usage statistics.

A sort routine will take about fifty man days to develop from a published algorithm, and a comprehensive print spooler (with stationery line-up and page reprint facilities) about eighty man days for an experienced systems programmer. Further time may be needed to set up transaction file management (opening new files fragments directories and degrades response time — it is better to rename existing files).

5. *Purchased and supplied software.*   Special software may be purchased for the system: system software such as a transaction processing monitor or a file handling package; application software to solve all or part of the problem. The software must

be checked and guidelines prepared before it can be used by the application programmers. A mechanism is required for recording software releases and patches, and notifying the software supplier of any problems. Other software which will be needed includes account number and password mechanisms, system housekeeping and report generators.

Communications protocols to be acquired and checked may include methods for driving remote printers or remote work stations, remote job entry, message switching, network access and access to remote files.

6. *Programming conventions.* Programming hints and conventions contribute to uniformity of program structure and help programmers to avoid gross inefficiency. Standards should exist for documentation, structure and layout with prohibitions and guides to improved efficiency.

Standard program skeletons should exist for the common 'difficult' areas:

— match, merge, update;
— page printing;
— analysis reports.

Examples of programming standards (both COBOL and BASIC Plus) and of program skeletons, can be found in the author's book *A guide to the successful management of computer projects.*

It would be a daunting task to prepare all of these common functions from scratch — and one which would call into question the viability of the project. In practice few projects will be put live with fewer than 100 man days of software of this nature, but 200 days should be a working maximum. More than this level means that a stable base does not exist for applications software development.

Using standard packages

Instinctively the idea of buying standard packaged systems looks attractive. For every user to write his own payroll package, for example, must be an enormous national waste of effort. And yet few packages have been successful. Those that have, tend to be in the more structured areas like linear programming, statistics or payroll where the rules are explicit and there is little room for discretion. Where discretion is the essence of the business (e.g. selling methods and thus order processing) it is not at all surprising to find packages are less applicable. At best a standard package is a solution to somebody else's problem — and should be judged in that light.

Standard packages fall into three main groups:

— *functional* packages (such as data entry, data management and report generators);
— *problem-solving* packages (such as linear programming, statistics, simulation and forecasting);
— *application* packages (such as payroll, nominal ledger, purchase ledger, sales ledger, costing, stock control and order processing).

Functional packages and problem-solving packages are a great deal easier to buy than application packages. Assuming the requirement is known it is a fairly straightforward matter to find out whether it is met or not. Application packages are difficult because of the nuances of business practice — and the problem that **the man with the business knowledge is seldom trained in systems analysis.**

At the same time the pressure to buy standard packages is increasing. The availability of inexpensive minicomputers means that the larger organisation can consider buying a system to support a single application — sales ledger perhaps, or order processing. It may be that where the volumes are sufficient there is little cost difference between one large machine and a number of dedicated smaller machines — particularly if a knotty business problem can be solved more quickly using a standard package.

The larger organisation may be looking for quick results in a specialised area but the same need is evident in smaller organisations — but usually for a different reason. The smaller organisation cannot justify the cost and risk associated with developing its application programs from scratch. Even if they knew exactly what they wanted (which is improbable with a first-time user) it is unlikely that they could improve on many of the application packages which are now available on the market.

Buyers can confidently expect to find packaged on-line systems in the areas of payroll, sales ledger, purchase ledger and nominal ledger on minicomputers (mainframe packages up to now have been more batch-oriented). Payroll systems available on stand-alone minicomputers cover all the usual payment methods — hourly, weekly and monthly paid with payment by cash, cheque or credit transfer. The best sales ledger systems combine open item and aged balance methods with on-line cash matching. Purchase ledger systems include purchase analysis while nominal ledgers can include accruals and sophisticated management reporting.

Choosing the package

Here then are the guidelines for choosing a package:

1. *Identify the job to be done.*   Write down what happens now in the system under review — note particularly:

   — volumes at every stage;
   — essential elements of the solution;
   — desirable elements;
   — particular needs of our business;
   — exceptions and how they are dealt with;
   — processing controls, progress chasing and queries.

   In this process, always distinguish 'method' from 'purpose'. When a system is first set up the purpose is clear and the constraints of method may be 20 per cent or so of the solution. Over a period of time the original purpose becomes less and less clear and the system becomes method dominated — 'we have always done it this way'. Our aim should be to solve the business problem well, not to perpetuate existing methods.

2. *Identify the packages available.*   A list of potential packages can be obtained from a variety of sources:

   — published software directories;
   — trade associations;
   — computer user groups;
   — software houses;
   — manufacturers;
   — personal recommendation.

   The last two categories are the ones to be viewed with most caution. Generally computer manufacturers are not in the application software business — so the best they can do is to offer you another organisation's solution to the problem (which probably will not have been designed with flexibility and change in mind).
   Personal recommendation means something if the system has been installed and running for a year or so — but too often the

recommendation is made in the 'honeymoon period' (after placing the order and before getting delivery).

Generally it is possible to reduce the list to a short-list (of up to three) by comparing the package with the business need followed by a visit to an installation. The short-list consists of packages which exist, which have been installed for over twelve months and which at least work to their own specification. **Any packages which 'nearly' work have to be rejected.** The supplier will be too busy making them work at the first site to give any attention to your needs. Check also that the package is written around a standard, current, fully supported operating system in a standard high-level language. Otherwise you will be vulnerable to the problems of growth and change.

3. *Match selected packages against needs.*   The selected package or packages can now be compared point by point with the statement of business requirements. It is not necessary — nor is it likely — that the package will satisfy every need exactly. For example, while looking for a purchase ledger system there may be a requirement to register all invoices received. The purchase ledger package may however assume that all invoices entered have first been approved (there are good reasons why this should be so). A feasible solution would be a manual invoice register with the package taking over once the invoices are approved for payment.

What is necessary is that a way can be seen to satisfy the business needs by the system as a whole — of which the package is only a (significant) part — also that it is reliable in operation.

Here are the areas to examine particularly:

—   are the *processing controls* good enough to continue considering this package? If tight input and processing controls have not been built in from the start it will be expensive to install them later and too risky not to. Is there an adequate audit trail?

—   has the package been designed to take advantage of *on-line input and interrogation?* Converted batch systems are not likely to be as good as a purpose-built on-line system; an unconverted batch system will probably have excessively high running costs. Is it convenient to use with well designed screens? Will it fit into the workflow?

—   are the *differences small enough* between the package and the business need to continue considering the package? Identify all modifications which will be required

— as a rule of thumb every program change takes two man days. If there are many essential modifications then the risk of failure is increased and the less relevant is the package.

— will it be *reliable in operation?* What happens if there is a hardware failure? Does it in fact involve unknown hardware, languages or operating systems? What are the recovery procedures following a failure?

— what limitations exist for *growth and change?* Is every existing document produced in some way by the package — including an adequate reserve for increased volumes/customers/products? Will it work in our existing hardware environment?

— is there adequate *documentation and training* available? How will the package be supported in the field? Is the supplier fully equipped or is the knowledge in a single individual (who has now left)?

4. *Carry out detailed testing.* Ideally the package should be installed as it exists and any changes made after it has bedded in and several months' experience has been gained. Initial testing should also be based on the original package — testing a modified package is like trying to hit a moving target. Prepare a representative set of static data (customers, products, suppliers, etc.) and a full range of transaction types. Set up the files using the package at a test site and test it systematically along the following lines:

— static data testing (open, close, amend master records, test file conversion);

— input transaction testing (type by type and in combination through to the file update);

— procedure testing (back end reports and suites);

— volume and date testing (test extremes of volume and advance the calendar over month, February, quarter and year end);

— restart/recovery testing.

Obtain a full set of printouts and check them:

— for accuracy;

— against current practice;

— against the business need.

As a result of this testing you will be able to answer the questions:

— where must the package be changed to meet my business need?
— where should my current business methods be changed to take advantage of the package?

There may seem to be a lot of work here but it will have to be done before going live. So why not do it before ordering the package?

5. *Carry out cost/benefit analysis.*   All the way through the evaluation process the user will have some sort of subjective feel for the relative costs and benefits involved. But subjective views are often wrong. We are looking for the best overall solution in terms of cost, quality and efficiency. It may be therefore that an apparently expensive package has the lowest 'whole life' cost, if the system is viewed as a whole (but not always).
    In the cost equation we must consider:

— hardware cost and installation;
— hardware support (if this is an unfamiliar machine) and maintenance;
— package cost;
— package support and maintenance;
— cost of essential modifications to the package;
— changes to existing organisation and procedures;
— clerical and operating costs;

and compare these costs with the cost of the existing system.
    To assess less tangible benefits (improved quality, fewer errors, faster turnround) the best guidelines can be obtained by looking closely at the experience of existing users.

6. *Implementation time-scale.*   Persuasive salesmen will tell you that their packages can be wheeled in and they will work immediately. While this is possible, it is unwise to take such a risk in any significant part of the business operation.
    Here are the implementation activities which must be followed when installing any new system (package or bespoke):

— system test original package, system test with modifications;

- write manual procedures, revise forms;
- write operating procedures;
- order equipment, install and commission;
- specify, program and test interfaces to related systems;
- specify, program and test file conversion procedures;
- review organisation structure, staff training;
- prepare and run user acceptance tests, get auditors' approval;
- parallel run old and new systems;
- go live on new system;
- close down old system.

These activities suggest a time-scale of six months at least — and pressure to go faster 'to solve an immediate problem' should be resisted. The immediate problem will not get better and if short cuts are taken it might get a great deal worse.

It is unlikely that any package will match the existing business exactly — we have seen that in some ways it may be better, in other ways it will be worse. However, a sense of perspective is required as even tailored in-house solutions have been known to have their faults.

Summary

It is better for programmers to arrive late on a project rather than early. All systems benefit from a little longer in the planning and gestation phase — but it is difficult to avoid giving idle programmers 'some work to get started on'. Far better to think the whole project through; to identify common functions and prepare them in advance (write them twice if necessary to get them really good); to identify common types of program and schedule them together (so that knowledge and techniques can be exploited); and to buy standard packages wisely as an aid to overall productivity.

9 Performance characteristics

The five main components of an on-line system are the terminals, the lines, the memory, the CPU and the file storage. Because the system is on-line, it must cope adequately with random processing requests — unlike a batch system in which the processor itself initiates the next request.

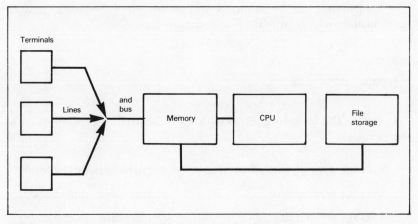

Figure 9.1 Components in the queuing system

Because of the random arrival of processing requests from many different sources, queues can build up. On a lightly loaded system there is not much of a problem but as the system becomes more heavily loaded queues build up and response time can degrade alarmingly fast.

The theory of queues is limited by what is mathematically practical. It is also constrained by the difficulty in forecasting the

various parameters with any accuracy. For any potential queue we
are interested in three processes:

— the input process;
— the service mechanism;
— the queue discipline.

A moment's thought will show how difficult these processes can be to
forecast or model.

— the *input process* is neither random nor constant; it is somewhere
  in between as, for example, the response time of the computer
  tends to affect the next action;
— the *service mechanism* is constant for a CPU (which acts as a
  single server) but operators at terminals have less predictable
  behaviour. They tend to work faster when there is more work to
  be done; they also tire by the end of the day;
— the *queuing discipline* is likely to be first-in-first-out but may
  also include a fair share scheduler, a priority system and maybe
  pre-emptive priorities as well.

By simplifying the problem it is possible to draw some general
conclusions which provide sound design guidelines.

Queuing principles

We define the following terms which will be used to explain queuing
principles:

Average arrival rate of messages $= \lambda$ (messages per second)

Average service rate $= \mu$ (messages per second)

Average service time $= S$ $= \dfrac{1}{\mu}$ (seconds per message)

Average utilisation $= \dfrac{\lambda}{\mu}$ $= \varrho$ (between 0 and 1)

So if messages arrive at one per second and are processed at two per
second:
$$\lambda = 1, \mu = 2, S = 0.5. \varrho = 0.5$$

Given the ration ϱ it is possible to establish the average queue length and the average queuing time (waiting time plus serving time) for random arrivals.

$$\text{Average } \textit{queue length, } n = \frac{\varrho}{1 - \varrho}$$

For x per cent of the time the probability is that the queue will not exceed:

$$- n.\log\left(\frac{100 - x}{100}\right) \text{ in length.}$$

Figure 9.2 shows the average *queue length* plotted for various values of ϱ together with the 90th and 95th percentiles. The queue will be as high as the 90th percentile on one occasion in ten — as high as the 95th percentile on one occasion in twenty. It can be seen that by the time $\varrho = 0.5$ the average queue length is one — and it begins to rise rapidly as ϱ increases.

Figure 9.3 show the *queuing time* for different values of ϱ. The queuing time is expressed in units of service time and the formula in this case is:

$$\textit{Queuing time} \text{ in multiples of service time}$$

$$\frac{q}{S} = \frac{\text{Average queue length}}{\varrho} = \frac{1}{1 - \varrho}$$

Once again the curve of average values is shown together with the 90th and 95th percentiles.

The graphs in Figures 9.2 and 9.3 assume completely random arrivals of processing requests. In practice the position is usually not quite so bad. Clerks tend to work on batches of work and the computer processes jobs at a constant rate. A revised formula for the queue length (known as the Erlang distribution with parameter m) is :

$$\text{Average queue length} = \frac{1}{2}\left(1 + \frac{1}{m}\right)\frac{\varrho}{1 - \varrho}$$

where m is a measure of randomness. If $m = 1$ we are back to our random distribution formula; if $m = \infty$ the formula represents a constant distribution.

Figure 9.4 shows the average queue size for $m = 1$ (random), 2, 5, and ∞ (constant). Although the actual distribution will lie between the extremes it is wise to take the upper value (as a form of safety factor). Generally 0.6 is the highest practical design value for ϱ and an example will illustrate why.

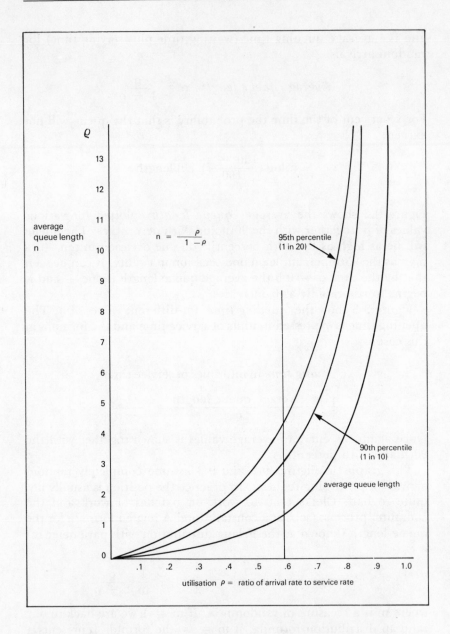

Figure 9.2 Average queue length for different utilisation ratios

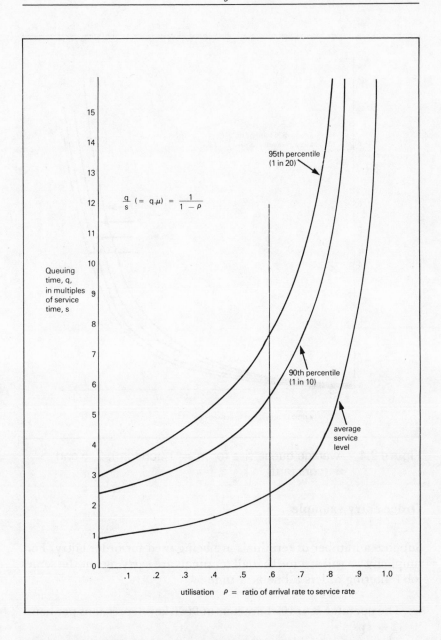

$$\frac{q}{s} \; (= q.\mu) = \frac{1}{1 - \rho}$$

Queuing time, q, in multiples of service time, s

95th percentile (1 in 20)

90th percentile (1 in 10)

average service level

utilisation ρ = ratio of arrival rate to service rate

Figure 9.3   Average queuing time per unit service time for different utilisation ratios

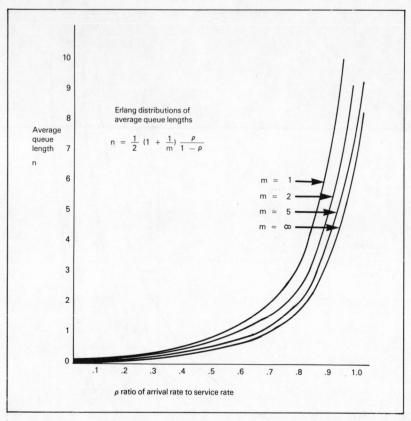

Figure 9.4   Average queue size for m = 1 (random), 2, 5 and ∞ (constant)

Order entry example

Suppose a number of terminals are being used for order entry. For simplicity we will assume that all terminals are carrying out the same job (entering orders a line at a time).

— The operator *keys* 10 characters at 9000 key depressions per hour (2½ cps);
— There is no *thinking time;*
— The input characters are *transmitted*;
— *Processing time* is entirely disc bound, and requires six disc accesses at, say, twelve data transfers per second;
— The results are *transmitted back* (50 characters) and are displayed.

Characters	Keying time (secs) at 9000 kd/h	Transmission time (secs) at 2400 baud
10	4	–
20	8	0.1
50	20	0.2
100	40	0.4
200	80	0.8
500	–	2.1
1000	–	4.2

Figure 9.5 Table of keying and transmission times

We thus have the following times (using Figure 9.5):

keying	4.0	
thinking	0	
transmission in	0	
queuing time	q	(waiting and servicing)
transmission back	0.2	
	4.2 + q	

Queuing time (q) is a function of the servicing time and the service ratio (ϱ); and the service ratio is itself a function of the queuing time (the longer the response, the longer before the next arrival).

Generally we thus have:

$$\varrho = \frac{\text{arrival rate}}{\text{service rate}} = \frac{j}{(k + q)} \cdot \frac{1}{\mu} \qquad (1)$$

and:

$$q = \frac{1}{\mu} \cdot \frac{1}{(1 - \varrho)} \quad \text{or} \quad \varrho = 1 - \frac{1}{\mu q} \qquad (2)$$

where: j = number of jobs
k = keyboard, thinking and transmission time (4.2 secs)
q = queuing time (waiting plus servicing)
μ = service rate (2 per second)

These two equations can be solved for either ϱ or q. It is simplest to solve for q and to obtain ϱ from (2).

$$\text{If} \qquad b = 1 + j - \mu k$$

$$\text{then} \qquad q = \frac{b + \sqrt{b^2 + 4\mu k}}{2\mu} \qquad (3)$$

Table 9.1 gives ϱ and q for various values of j in our example:

Table 9.1

No. of jobs (j)	ϱ	q	time per txn (secs) (k + q)	time for 100 txns (secs) 100 (k + q)/j
4	0.39	0.83	5.03	125.8
6	0.56	1.14	5.34	89.0
8	0.69	1.61	5.81	72.6
10	0.78	2.24	6.44	64.4

As the number of jobs increases so does the response time. Once ϱ becomes greater than 0.6 (about seven terminals in our example) the law of diminishing returns applies. Adding more terminals increases the waiting time at a faster rate than overall time is reduced.

In this example we assumed that twelve disc transfers per second was the working maximum. In practice this figure is a function of the discs being used, the amount of program swapping or paging and the transfer rate. Following our queuing rule it is wise to assume that the maximum access rate is 0.6 times the theoretical maximum. Discs with an average access time of 45 m secs (seek, latency and transfer) thus have a working maximum of thirteen transfers per second. In practice it is not difficult to set up the test described and to see the effect of adding more terminals (and of running a background printing job). It is of course important to use realistic files and the genuine file access method, for access times are misleading on small files (even if the right access method is used).

The table in Figure 9.6 contains a summary of the values we have looked at so far. Queue size and multiples of average service time are shown for values of the distribution ratio, ϱ, up to 0.9 together with values for the 90th and 95th percentiles. Note that queuing time is the sum of the waiting time and service time and is expressed in units of service time (1/service rate μ). The figures in the table are useful for simple queuing situations but where there is a loop (rate of arrivals depends on rate of response), as in our order entry example, the BASIC program of Figure 9.7 may be used. This program was devised by John Sharp of Hill Samuel and takes account of additional factors e.g. swapping time, block mode data entry (buffered screen) or single character data entry. The program can be used on the same order entry example to illustrate the effect of program swapping. The user space in this example is 64k words and the job space 12k words — so swapping commences when more than five terminals are using the system. The results are summarised in Table 9.2 and the output for six concurrent users shown in detail in Figure 9.8

Utilisation ratio ϱ		0.1	0.2	0.3	0.4	0.5	0.6	0.7	0.8	0.9
Queue size $n = \dfrac{\varrho}{1-\varrho}$	Average	.11	.25	.43	.67	1.0	1.5	2.3	4.0	9
	1 in 10	.25	.58	1.0	1.5	2.3	3.5	5.3	9.2	21
	1 in 20	.33	.75	1.3	2.0	3.0	4.5	6.9	12.0	27
Queuing time in multiples of service time $\dfrac{q}{s} = q \cdot \mu = \dfrac{1}{1-\varrho}$	Average	1.1	1.3	1.4	1.7	2.0	2.5	3.3	5.0	10
	1 in 10	2.5	3.0	3.2	3.8	4.6	5.8	7.6	11.5	23
	1 in 20	3.3	3.9	4.2	5.1	6.0	7.5	10.0	15.0	30

Figure 9.6   Table to determine queue size and queuing time for different utilisation ratios

Table 9.2

No. of jobs	ϱ	q	swap	time per txn $(k + q)$secs	time for 100 txns $100(k + q)/j$ secs
4	0.39	0.83	0	5.07	126.8
6	0.59	1.31	0.04	5.56	92.7
8	0.73	2.22	0.09	6.47	80.9
10	0.81	3.41	0.13	7.66	76.6

```
QUEUE   15:28              11-May-79
1000 READ M,RO,R6,R1,R7,R3,R4
1010 DATA 64,2.5,240,0,0,250,45
1020 PRINT "SYSTEM PARAMETERS"
1030 PRINT "USER CORE               :";M
1040 PRINT "KEYING RATE (CPS)       :";RO
1050 PRINT "DISPLAY RATE (CPS)      :";R6
1060 PRINT "CPU TIME/INPUT CH(MS)   :";R1
1070 PRINT "CPU TIME/OUTPUT CH(MS)  :";R7
1080 PRINT "SWAP TIME (MSECS)       :";R3
1090 PRINT "DISC ACESS TIME (MSECS) :";R4
1900 PRINT
2000 READ J,K,XO,X1,X4,X5,X6,X7,X8
2010 DATA 6,12,10,1,6,50,50,0,0
2020 PRINT "TRANSACTION PARAMETERS"
2030 PRINT "NUMBER OF JOBS          :";J
2040 PRINT "JOB SIZE (K)            :";K
2050 PRINT "INPUT CHS               :";XO
2060 PRINT "DIRECT(0) OR BUFFER(1)  :";X1
2070 PRINT "DISC ACESSES            :";X4
2080 PRINT "PROCESSOR TIME (MSECS)  :";X5
2090 PRINT "DISPLAY CHS             :";X6
2100 PRINT "THINK TIME (SECS)       :";X7
2110 PRINT "DISPLAY/THINK OVERLAP(%):";X8
2900 PRINT
3000 X3=1-INT(M/K)/J
3010 IF X3>0 THEN 3030
3020 X3=0
3030 TO=XO/RO
3040 T1=X1*XO/R6
3050 T3=R3*X3/1000
3060 T4=(R4/0.6)*X4/1000
3070 T5=(X5+XO*(R1+R7*(1-X1))+X6*R7)/1000
3080 T6=X6/R6
3090 T7=X7-T6*X8/100
3100 U=1/(T3+T4+T5)
3110 T8=TO+T1+T6+T7
3120 B=1+J-U*T8
3130 Q=(B+SQR(B*B+4*U*T8))/(2*U)
3140 T9=T8+Q
3150 L=J/T9
3160 T2=Q-(1/U)
3500 PRINT "SERVICE RATE",U
3510 PRINT "ARRIVAL RATE",L
3520 PRINT "UTILISATION "L/U
3530 P$="\            \    ###.##        ###.##"
3900 PRINT
4000 PRINT "ACTION          TIME           %"
4010 PRINT USING P$,"KEYING",TO,TO*100/T9
4020 PRINT USING P$, "TRANSMIT",T1,T1*100/T9
4030 PRINT USING P$, "WAIT",T2,T2*100/T9
4040 PRINT USING P$, "SWAP",T3,T3*100/T9
4050 PRINT USING P$, "DISC",T4,T4*100/T9
4060 PRINT USING P$, "PROCESS",T5,T5*100/T9
4070 PRINT USING P$, "DISPLAY",T6,T6*100/T9
4080 PRINT USING P$, "THINK",T7,T7*100/T9
4090 PRINT USING P$, "TOTAL",T9
4900 PRINT
4990 P1$="###          ###.##"
5000    PRINT "  %        RESPONSE TIME    MEAN";Q
5010 FOR X=10 TO 90 STEP 10
5020 PRINT USING P1$,X,-Q*LOG((100-X)/100)
5030 NEXT X
5040 PRINT \PRINT
32767   END
```

Figure 9.7 BASIC program

```
QUEUE    15:27            11-May-79
SYSTEM PARAMETERS
USER CORE                 :  64
KEYING RATE (CPS)         :  2.5
DISPLAY RATE (CPS)        :  240
CPU TIME/INPUT CH(MS)     :  0
CPU TIME/OUTPUT CH(MS)    :  0
SWAP TIME (MSECS)         :  250
DISC ACESS TIME (MSECS)   :  45

TRANSACTION PARAMETERS
NUMBER OF JOBS            :  6
JOB SIZE (K)             :  12
INPUT CHS                :  10
DIRECT(0) OR BUFFER(1)    :  1
DISC ACESSES             :  6
PROCESSOR TIME (MSECS)    :  50
DISPLAY CHS              :  50
THINK TIME (SECS)        :  0
DISPLAY/THINK OVERLAP(%) :  0

SERVICE RATE    1.84615
ARRIVAL RATE    1.08005
UTILISATION     .585026

ACTION        TIME          %
KEYING        4.00         72.00
TRANSMIT      0.04          0.75
WAIT          0.76         13.75
SWAP          0.04          0.75
DISC          0.45          8.10
PROCESS       0.05          0.90
DISPLAY       0.21          3.75
THINK         0.00          0.00
TOTAL         5.56

%        RESPONSE TIME     MEAN 1.3053
10           0.14
20           0.29
30           0.47
40           0.67
50           0.90
60           1.20
70           1.57
80           2.10
90           3.01
```

Figure 9.8   Output for six concurrent users

It can be seen that although swapping time is not very high in itself it increases the utilisation ratio appreciably (in this example) and thus the time per transaction — see the similar figures without swapping in Table 9.1.

Bottleneck areas

Bottlenecks may occur at a variety of points in the system — at the terminals, on the communication lines, in memory capacity, in CPU capacity and in disc accesses. Some of the problems can be anticipated, others can be alleviated. The key is to get the basic capacities right at the start — fine tuning is of limited use if the solution is strategically too tight. We will look first at some basic ways of improving throughput — then draw some general conclusions.

Terminal capacity should be calculated using the methods shown for peak volumes. It is quite legitimate to approximate and to consider an 'average' job. There must be enough terminals for peak rate working (including spares) and to process two heavy days in one (following equipment failure for example).

Although the CPU is a 'single server', a number of terminals form a multiple server system. The theory here is more complex than for a single server but there is one general rule for the designer to observe — a number of specilialised terminals (servers) may give a better service to a particular class of customer, but the overall service level will be worse than with an equivalent number of all-purpose terminals. This type of situation may arise with telephoned orders in particular. It can be quite a difficult decision to weigh up the advantages of organising staff by product group/customer group against the additional cost of providing such a service (it may require twice as many staff and terminals).

Problems of this nature are best modelled by simulation methods. Random arrivals and random servicing times can be generated from random numbers which are translated into an arrival distribution by formula or table look up. An example of such a distribution with a pronounced mean and long tail is illustrated in Figure 9.9.

Line capacity may be a problem with remote terminals. It may be necessary to carry out local concentration, or to hold screen and print formats locally, or to carry out local editing. The implications of line failure need to be considered — will back up on the switched network be adequate?

Seconds between arrivals	Random numbers										
0	00	01									
1	02	03	04	05							
2	06	07	08	09	10	11	12	13			
3	14	15	16	17	18	19	20	21	22	23	24	25
4	26	27	28	29	30	31	32	33	34		
5	35	36	37	38	39	40	41				
6	42	43	44	45	46	47					
7	48	49	50	51	52						
8	53	54	55	56	57						
9	58	59	60	61							
10	62	63	64	65							
11	66	67	68	69							
12	70	71	72								
13	73	74	75								
14	76	77	78								
15	79	80	81								
16	82	83									
17	84	85									
18	86	87									
19	88	89									
20	90	91									
21	92	93									
22	94										
23	95										
24	96										
25	97										
26	98										
27	99										

The numbers 00 to 99 generated at random create the distribution shown, which has a mean of 8.89. So, for example, the random number 64 generates an arrival interval of 10 seconds; the random number 31 generates an arrival interval of 4 seconds.

Figure 9.9 Generating a distribution of arrivals from random numbers

Unbuffered interfaces to the bus may cause data characters to be lost when the bus loading becomes heavy. Buffered multiplexers overcome the problem and may give the additional benefit of direct memory access (DMA).

Lack of *memory capacity* can stop a system faster than almost anything else. There must be sufficient basic capacity so that the swapping or paging overhead is acceptable. Capacity can be improved by writing smaller programs, by splitting large programs, by sharing common code or by getting more memory.

CPU capacity can be improved by offloading work on to buffered terminals and intelligent terminals, by using buffered input/output multiplexers, by adding cache memory and by rewriting inefficient code.

Disc accesses are limited by the speed of the CPU and the bus. Disc utilisation can be improved by reducing head movement (intelligent splitting of files over two drives, by faster swapping (using swapping discs or swapping core), by keeping file directories well organised, by choice of file access method or by going for faster discs (maybe needing a faster CPU)).

All areas can be improved by seeking 'parallelism'. If applications can be split on to a number of (smaller) machines and run in parallel the dangers of being overloaded on a single machine are greatly reduced.

Summary

It can be seen that the greatest risk comes from the high-volume application which cannot be spread over a period of time and which cannot be spread over more than one machine. With such an application the strategy must be to go for a machine which:

— is large enough for the current peak load;
— can process two heavy days' work in one day;
— is not at the limit of its specification;
— allows an upward growth path without rewriting software.

These guidelines are needed for a whole variety of reasons — because there will be business growth; because new applications will emerge; because there needs to be a reserve for equipment failure; and also because traffic forecasting is a difficult business. By playing safe all that is risked is a little hardware expense — not the success of the project.

10 Reliability, security and control

Distributed processing not only brings computer power into the work place, it ensures the computer becomes an integral part of the workflow. But this harnessing of the power of the computer to help the business has its dangers as well. If the computer system breaks down there is a risk that all associated work stops. Systems designers must therefore pay particular attention to system availability; and to ways of keeping the system running, of minimising the risks from any failure and of recovering smoothly.

Aircraft blind-landing systems achieve guaranteed reliability by having most computer components triplicated — the cost is warranted because of the penalties of failure. Few businesses can justify triplication of all components and an acceptable degree of reliability can be achieved with only a few redundant components. In this chapter we will examine the problem under the following headings:

— ways of achieving reliability and availability;
— designing for speedy recovery;
— checklist of system controls;
— guidelines for security and privacy;
— precautions against physical risks;
— disaster procedures.

Reliability and availability

Reliability has to be considered in the system design in the same way that user needs and system performance are designed in. The points to consider are in the checklist of Figure 10.1 which is expanded below.

Modularity of design means that faults can be identified, isolated and the risk of total failure reduced. The concept of modularity applies to hardware (a number of processors rather than one all-purpose monster) and software (integration is the word to avoid). Modularity forces the designer to define the interfaces between systems clearly. It thus encourages project implementation in stages and provides the opportunity to profit from the lessons of early stages (reducing the overall risk of failure).

Duplication of components means that if a fault develops, the systems can be kept working with a small (maybe invisible) delay for the user. To have systems standing by, *idle,* waiting for the prime system to fail is both expensive and ill-advised. Far better to split the workload so that less critical jobs are on the standby machine (and maybe the whole work could be put on one machine at a pinch). A standby system which is seldom used always seems to fail at the moment it is called into service.

'Hot standby' is also more difficult than 'warm standby'. Hot standby means systems that are duplicated and come into operation automatically in the event of a failure. The problem is to detect the failure, isolate it and to call in the standby mechanism. It is far easier, and generally acceptable, to switch processors manually and to restart within fifteen to thirty minutes.

If there are two processors, ensure that the printers and VDUs can be switched from one to another so that there is maximum overall reliability. The printer failing should not bring down the whole system.

Back-up systems may be in-house if the number of machines or the risk justifies it. Alternatively, a compatible service bureau may be used for backup. **Some form of back-up must be available for all significant on-line systems.** If a local bureau is to be used it will mean installing modems and giving thought to compatibility. The account numbers should be the same for both systems (but the passwords different, of course) and both using the same release of the operating system.

Back-up systems include:

— standby generators (in case of power failure) of sufficient power

and with voltage stabilising equipment;
— dial-up lines as back-up to any leased lines;
— alternative means of processing peak loads.

Fall-back methods are generally needed for real-time systems and on-line systems which are being recovered after a failure. There must be some way of carrying on the business until the computer systems are brought back up. Establish with the user what level and duration of failure can be tolerated. For example, cash dispensers normally used on-line may be able to carry on working after a line failure — if they always contain a current list of cardholders who may *not* be given cash.

When designing fall-back methods here are the methods to consider:

— periodic dumping of files to microfiche (combining a historical record with a standby reference source);
— overnight printing of current status (for daytime reference as well as standby);
— regular printing of key running totals (maybe half-hourly so that the figures do not take long to be brought up to date manually);
— continuous printing of transactions and control totals (so that the work done can be readily identified).

A low degree of innovation in the project is a positive aid to reliability. New methods, new equipment, new combinations of equipment and new software will all cause problems during project development and on into live running. When a product (including a program) is first built, it is a prototype, nothing more. We can always find ways of doing the job better a second time and of making the product more robust. So limit the degree of innovation in the project and **never base the design on newly announced products.**

A low degree of computer operator intervention during processing improves running times and reduces errors from incorrect responses. On-line systems are, by definition, run by the terminal and without operator intervention. It is less easy, on minicomputers, to run batch jobs in sequence without the operator initiating every one. One typical installation was able to reduce its end-of-day running time by 25 per cent by chaining these batch programs together and providing default responses to all questions. When the operator was needed, the console sounded an alarm to attract his attention.

Control of program releases reduces the risk of failure from new and possibly ill-tested new program versions. Programmers should not be able to get their programs into production, nor should they be able to modify production programs directly. A mechanism is needed to control the release of new versions and to issue the new versions simultaneously to all sites. In particular software releases need to be co-ordinated so that all the various sites in the network are in step with each other.

Preventive maintenance on a regular cycle is required if equipment failures are to be avoided. And if the equipment does fail, the servicing engineer should be encouraged to fix the fault for good — not to fix it as quickly as possible. Encourage the engineer to take a little longer, becuse it will save him and you a lot of second visits. This attitude is difficult to maintain in the pressure of keeping the business running and needs to be communicated to all staff likely to deal with the engineer.

Finally, *simplicity of design* is a strategy for reliability. Complex products do not have the inherent reliability of simple products — and what is worse, problems take longer to detect and are likely to have unforeseeable implications. Keeping it simple and developing the implementation progressively make reliability more probable and allow easier recovery when mistakes are made.

- Modularity of design
- Duplication of components
- Back-up systems available
- Fall-back methods developed
- Low degree of innovation
- Low degree of computer operator intervention
- Control of program releases
- Regular preventive maintenance
- Simplicity of design

Figure 10.1   Reliability checklist

System recovery

Recovery from failure is all too often an afterthought which is considered during system testing or maybe not until after a failure. In practice there are three types of recovery to be considered:

— transmission failure;
— irretrievable loss of a disc;
— power failure.

By paying attention to these points during the design much can be done to aid recovery at no great cost.

A *failure in transmission* between two processors is such a probable event that recovery routines are built into all but the simplest protocols. As was explained in Chapter 4, the transmitting processor calculates a check character for every message block, which is transmitted with the block. The receiving processor re-computes the check character and if the result is in any way different, requests retransmission. To ensure that no block is missed completely the receiver acknowledges successive blocks in different ways (alternately ACK 0 and ACK 1 in the 2780 BSC protocol).

Because data transmission is a clearly defined task which is application independent it is possible to define a straightforward recovery method. Every block is treated as a 'checkpoint' from which recovery can take place. At any time we know the message has been transmitted correctly up to the last correctly acknowledged block.

All methods of recovery are based on checkpoints. We need to be confident that we can recreate the state of the system at a given time and have the ability to get back to an up-to-date position.

Irretrievable *loss of a disc* may occur through hardware failure or software corruption. The basic requirement then is to have a copy of the disc at a previously defined point which can be used to recreate the situation at the time of the failure. On a low-volume system it may be acceptable to re-enter the input (so long as it does not happen too often) but generally it is necessary to log the transactions (or an after image) so that recovery can be automatic (see Figure 10.2). By keeping today's transactions separate (and updating the transaction file in batch mode) recovery is speeded up considerably.

Many on-line systems have two disc drives and no tape drive so the way the files are located is clearly important. As a general rule log files should not be on the same disc as the file being logged. Spool files should not be on the same disc as the files from which they are created. By organising the files in this way it is possible, for example, to print the spool file while recovering the corrupted disc or to recreate the spool files if it is that disc which has been lost.

Here then are the points to consider:

— a known good copy of the file must always exist;
— all transactions since the 'good copy' must be retained;
— on all but trivial jobs recovery should be 'automatic';

— keeping today's transactions in a separate file makes recovery easier;
— splitting the files over two discs may make recovery faster or less noticeable.

If a *power failure* or memory failure occurs it must be assumed that all current operations may be incomplete (and possibly data lost 'in flight'). In an order-processing application, for example, we know that the second item has been accepted and updated but how far has the third reached? Transaction logging will not solve the problem either (maybe the failure occurred between the update and the transaction log). What the transaction log does do is to allow recovery from a defined checkpoint.

As a minimum, such checkpoints are taken at the end of day and after any major (batch) event — completion of cash input, for example. Where recovery will take a long time, checkpoints must be built in as a more regular feature.

On-line system recovery

Recovery from the failure of an on-line system is always easier than that of a real-time system. On-line systems fall into two categories — batched input and single transaction input. With *batched input* the characteristics are:

— a given batch is entered from a single terminal;
— there may be several terminals working on different batches in parallel;
— main files are referenced but not updated.

The recovery approach following a failure is to run an 'audit' program which establishes which batches are complete (and verifies that they balance to their control totals). The program may go on to establish how far incomplete batches have reached (from records written to disc) and re-establish their controls. The operator is told where to re-start within the batch. Re-starting incomplete batches adds to the complexity of the recovery and it may well be acceptable to delete them and for the keyboard operator to start the batch again.

With *single transaction input* the characteristics are:

— there may be several terminals working on different transactions in parallel;

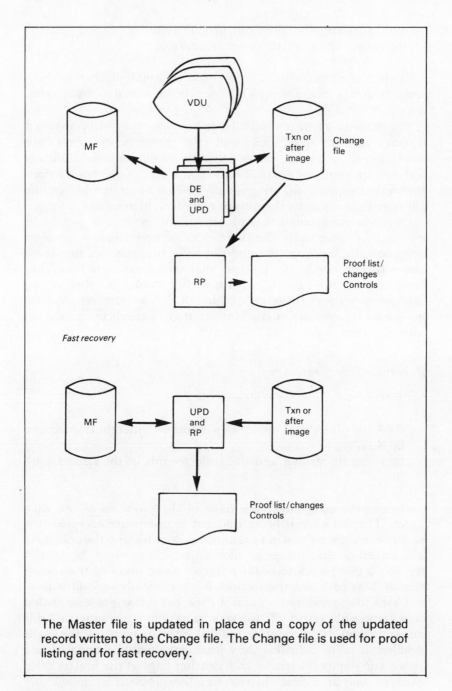

The Master file is updated in place and a copy of the updated record written to the Change file. The Change file is used for proof listing and for fast recovery.

Figure 10.2   Real-time updating

— main files are referenced but not updated;
— the transactions update common controls.

This class of problem includes a single terminal which references and updates a mainfile which is not being updated from other terminals.

The recovery approach is similar to batched input. All completed transactions are identified and the common controls are recalculated. It is good practice anyway to obtain serial numbers and update common controls only at the end of the transaction. Incomplete transactions are generally deleted but it may be possible partially to reconstruct them from records written to disc.

On most minicomputer and mainframe systems a degree of recovery is built into the hardware/software and is invoked automatically. Even so, running the audit program is a minimum post-recovery check. It is true that automatic roll-back/roll-forward procedures can work with on-line input, but they are an expensive overhead (in terms of additional disc transfers) and are not suited to minicomputers. Nor are they of much practical help with real-time input.

Real-time system recovery

With *real-time input* the characteristics are:

— there may be several terminals working on different transactions in parallel;
— they are all reading and updating records in the same master file.

Order processing illustrates many of the problems of real-time input. The stock file is being updated as orders are accepted, the order details are written out to the open order file and the orders are also logged on disc or tape to allow automatic recovery. Because of the way a given stock record is referenced and updated from many terminals as part of a transaction, it is technically very difficult to roll back to a known stable point. In practice it is safe to assume that it is impossible (short of two processors and an uninterruptable power supply). If processors at multiple sites are involved, the whole problem is more difficult. Every processor should be updated in a systematic sequence, setting and clearing flags as the update takes place or one at a time. In this way the problem is limited to a recovery on a maximum of two machines (bad enough in any case).

Recovery is easier (and may be made fully automatic) if the pseudo real-time approach is used (as in Figure 10.3). During order entry the mainfile is referenced but not updated. The updating is done by a single program which services all the input terminals and writes away transactions as they are complete. The advantage is easier recovery; the main disadvantage is the delay between query and update. By the time the update takes place the stock may have gone to another order. There is also some loss of efficiency with extra file accesses.

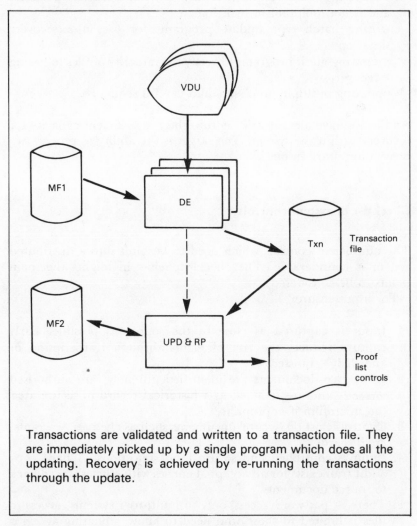

Transactions are validated and written to a transaction file. They are immediately picked up by a single program which does all the updating. Recovery is achieved by re-running the transactions through the update.

Figure 10.3 Pseudo real-time updating

In summary, the solution to be adopted depends on the problem to be solved but the points to consider are:

— logging transactions so that recovery is possible;
— taking regular checkpoints by backing up files to reduce re-start time (on large files take dumps less frequently and 'roll-forward' to create checkpoints);
— recognising that manufacturers' recovery software can help for on-line input and for roll-forward but has efficiency penalties and is not foolproof in real time;
— writing batch type update programs for use in a recovery situation;
— preparing audit programs to verify the integrity of files following a recovery;
— updating multiple processors in a careful sequence.

And as we have already said, ensure there is sufficient capacity for recovery within the system. The target is the ability to process two heavy days' work in one.

Checklist of system controls

The number of controls which need to be built into a distributed system is considerable. The checklist below highlights the main points to be considered.

For input ensure:

1. Input is captured as close to the source as possible. Early capture reduces the risk of errors through transcription or knowledge transfer.
2. All source documents are identified uniquely, are authorised correctly and are retained as a historical record in secure areas (on microfilm if appropriate).
3. Controls exist on 'secure' documents such as cheques, warrants, credit cards.
4. Input is controlled and so are input rejections. A hard copy audit trail exists for all accepted entries with entries traced back to source documents.
5. There is 'password access' only to multi-user systems; access to files is limited to those who need to know; updating access is further restricted. Change passwords on a regular basis.

6. Meaningful mnemonics are used rather than codes. Coding adds an unnecessary extra step and an additional source of error.
7. Input is vetted as close to the source as possible, using mainfiles to ensure accuracy. Accounting codes and analysis codes are checked for consistency with the input type.
8. Rejections are controlled carefully, also cancellations and reversals. Remember, error correction is very error prone.
9. Systems exist to prevent and detect duplicate, missing and unauthorised input — at any of the processing stages.

For processing ensure:

10. All data transmission is checked in some way. Transmitting everything twice (then comparing the results) is a simple and acceptable method for low volumes.
11. Methods exist to ensure the right files are used and the right program versions. Ensure there is control over releasing new programs and that all sites are updated.
12. Random access files are verified as often as they are saved. Sufficient generations of files and programs are held to allow recovery (five generations on daily systems, three generations on less frequently run systems).
13. Extra controls are instituted during file conversion to ensure balances are converted correctly with no duplicates and no omissions.
14. Programs which update mainfiles are kept to a minimum and control totals are printed following an update.
15. Checkpoints are taken sufficiently often to allow speedy recovery. Re-start/recovery routines are tested periodically and all work.

For output ensure:

16. Control of output covers — checking run controls, checking everything is present, carrying out final distribution and notifying user departments of any failures.
17. Systems exist for maintaining operator and user manuals. Copies of all project documentation and manuals are held in another building.

Security and privacy

There have been several hundred published cases of fraud in which computers have been involved and many of these cases have been well publicised. The problem, however, must be seen in perspective. In many of the cases the computer happened to be the accounting medium (rather than the main tool in the fraud) and a few hundred known cases is not many in comparison to the total amount of crime in business organisations.

If anything computers make most types of office crime more difficult because of the (hopefully) inbuilt controls, audit trails and relentless obeying of rules. That is not to say that line management can relax about security — they must look at computer security in many ways exactly as they look at systems security using manual methods or accounting machines. Distributed processing does require extra vigilance. A central computer complex, with expensive equipment, comprehensive master files and all the program code, clearly needs to be protected. It is easy to overlook cheap distributed computers, which are operated in an informal way and located in the office environment.

Security targets

To set up a secure system we need to identify first the likely targets. These targets fall into three groups:

— money;
— information;
— physical damage.

Precautions against physical risks are covered in the next part of this chapter. We shall for the moment restrict the discussion to the security of money (or payment instruments) and security of information. Privacy against *incorrect access* to information we shall group with security against the *incorrect use* of information.

We shall set out the areas of 'good practice' which are aimed at defeating both wilful and accidental breaches of security.

Abusing the system

When the target is money, in general the *system is used correctly but to the wrong ends.* An employee or an outsider uses the system to obtain money, payment instruments or goods for their own purposes. The counter measure here is to carry out a risk assessment of the system as a whole (of which the computer can be regarded as a black box) and to institute measures along the following lines:

1. Ensure all payment instructions are authorised by two people; that systems exist to check correct authorisation.
2. Examine particularly all areas where communications go out of the system/organisation. What is to prevent misuse of the system? Should controls be tighter above a certain payment value or to a certain type of customer?
3. Control the loading of new accounts and changing credit limits. Ensure all file insertions, changes, enquiries and deletions are listed out for examination by a supervisor.
4. Ensure audit trails exist so that every transaction can be traced back to its source and through to its completion. It must be possible to reconstruct what happened at least twelve months later.
5. Ensure system controls exist along the lines already described in this chapter. It must not be possible to duplicate, lose or corrupt data without it being detected.
6. Introduce additional controls at times of change. New systems do have errors and the errors are less likely to be discovered if any payments are made automatically.
7. Ensure system usage statistics are monitored to find out who is using the system, for what and when.

Above all, monitor all known threats and be clear on what happens if misconduct is detected. The knowledge of speedy discovery and retribution is a great deterrent.

Breaking the system

When the target is information, in general the *system is being used incorrectly for the wrong ends*. The problem is one of restricting access to system resources to those who have the need and the right of access. A problem of distributed systems is that in our desire to make them easy to use, we are also making them easy to break. Here are the guidelines to observe if security and privacy of information are to be maintained:

1. Use keyboard locks on terminals in public places. Use password access on multi-user systems and change passwords regularly. Identify transactions to the originating VDU and password.

2. Restrict physical access to computers to prevent accidental damage, misuse or vandalism.
3. Restrict the use of dial-up lines into the computer as far as possible. Connect incoming calls manually rather than providing automatic modem connection.
4. Keep the links between distributed and central computers as loose as possible. Carry out data transfers in RJE mode or by transfer of media (e.g. magnetic tape, floppy disc).
5. Use some form of authenticator or test key for all significant external instructions. Consider using encryption on key fields to disguise data content.
6. Limit access to files (or parts of files) depending on the 'need to know'. Control separately read-only access and updating access.
7. Limit replies to the essential minimum (i.e. the answer to a credit check is Yes or No, not the amounts involved).
8. Recognise the value of the software and program code. Ensure it is kept secure and changes cannot be released by the programmers.
9. Examine carefully the way individuals are identified. In future passwords will be replaced by more foolproof identification (e.g. voice pattern recognition).

We have seen already that a *high degree of interaction* between systems leads to problems of software complexity and recovery from failure. We now see they lead also to greater problems of security. It is perhaps just as well that the business need for them is not overwhelming.

Precautions against physical risks

The checklist below covers the main points to consider when looking at physical risks. The measures to be implemented depend on the degree of risk and the related consequential loss. For example, there will probably be different precautions at central and distributed sites.

Prevention/reduction measures

1. Carry out a thorough survey of the (proposed) computer location to identify risks from fire, flood and from accommodation defects.
2. Incorporate waterproof and fireproof/resistant (minimum one hour fire rating) doors, floors, ceiling and partitions/walls in design of computer area.

3. Install automatic fire extinguishing equipment with automatic power supply 'cut off'.
4. Provide suitable hand-operated fire extinguishers.
5. Provide water pumping equipment if appropriate.
6. Install appropriate air filtration, temperature and humidity control systems.
7. Install back-up generator (and an uninterruptible power supply for critical systems).
8. Provide methods for restricting access to computer and associated equipment — security locks on doors and windows, plus access control systems.
9. Restrict access to distributed computers and VDUs to prevent accidental damage, wilful damage or vandalism.
10. Ensure methods exist for 'policing' the site out of normal working hours.
11. Ensure buffer stocks of critical supplies.
12. Monitor staff morale — identify grievances.
13. Insist on regular maintenance of all computer and associated equipment and magnetic media.
14. Carry out a regular review and testing of control procedures.

Detection measures

1. Install smoke or heat detectors (perhaps linked to automatic alarm system to fire brigade).
2. Carry out a regular analysis of environment — air sampling.
3. Install water detectors in groundfloor and basement areas if appropriate.
4. Fit intruder alarms on doors and windows.
5. Monitor/record/analyse equipment and magnetic media fault reports.
6. Install electronic surveillance equipment for use during the time the building is empty.

Contingency plans

1. Ensure the availability of spare/back-up equipment capacity — consider duplicating major components (computer and associated plant).
2. Secure key records and files in an off-site back-up store — which must contain all items required to recreate latest master files and to run all systems at a back-up site (data files, program documentation, system and operating procedures, stationery and all supplies).
3. Prepare, implement and review detailed disaster procedures (covered in the next few pages).

4. Provide standby accommodation where appropriate with services (e.g. power supplies, lines) readily available to install new computer equipment in the event of total loss of the existing computer accommodation. The longest delays following a serious disaster are often caused by the problems of accommodation rather than problems of hardware replacement.

5. Ensure staff are fully conversant with all aspects of the counter measures and associated procedures — carry out regular tests and training.

6. Ensure spread of job knowledge — avoid 'one man' experts in any field of operation.

Insurance

Ensure adequate insurance cover for:

- hardware replacement (computer and associated equipment);
- reinstatement of data;
- increased cost of working;
- consequential loss.

Disaster control procedures

If a disaster should occur it is vital that the subsequent events are properly controlled to ensure a quick and accurate recovery. To achieve this the disaster control procedures must be clear and concise and be kept as simple as possible. They should act as a comprehensive checklist of action to be taken and should contain all the relevant information required. Complex procedures are unlikely to be actioned correctly.

The disaster procedures developed by Roger Moore and his staff at Hill Samuel are organised into seven 'stand-alone' sections:

1. Disaster Alert Procedures
2. Disaster Control Procedures
3. Disaster Assessment Procedures
4. Standby Site Contact Procedures
5. Standby Site Support Procedures
6. Standby Site Operating Procedures
7. Work Assessment Procedures

} All of these activities go on in parallel — reporting into and co-ordinated by Disaster Controller

As before, the disaster procedures for central sites are likely to be more comprehensive than those of distributed sites because of the risks involved and the difficulty of backing up a central site.

Disaster alert procedures

This section details the procedures to be followed to action a disaster alert.

Alarm is raised — clearly defines alarm procedure during normal working hours and at all other times.

Alarm is verified — it is important that a check for a false alarm is carried out.

Personnel on call-out list are alerted — this list is split into two groups:

— control personnel — management and senior operations staff;
— support personnel — other key staff required in immediate recovery situation.

Personnel report to the incident centre — it will greatly assist the disaster recovery programme if, as part of disaster planning, an óffice is designated to be used as an incident centre. This office could be part of the disaster store and similarly should be situated remotely from the computer installation. However, it must have good communication facilities, particularly telephones. In the event of a disaster alert all staff should report to the incident centre and not to the disaster scene to ensure proper control of the events following a disaster alert.

Disaster control procedures

Senior person assumes responsibility — action needs to be taken immediately to ensure proper control of events. Senior person assumes role of disaster controller.

Situation is reviewed — disaster controller establishes latest situation *re* disaster and staff contacted. He ensures that the remaining staff on call-out list are contacted and that a record is kept of who has been contacted and when. The disaster procedures should contain an up-to-date list of all relevant staff names, addresses and telephone numbers. This list should also include relevant details of:

— standby computer sites;
— all emergency services (fire, police, etc.);
— taxi companies (preferably radio-controlled);
— supplier support staff;
— all other appropriate staff, companies, contacts.

Responsibilities are assigned — disaster controller assigns appropriate personnel to each of the five remaining disaster procedure sections. He should ensure that they each have a copy of the relevant section of the procedures and that a record is kept of personnel deployment. The disaster procedures manual should be designed to allow each section to be removed easily and distributed. Copies of the disaster procedures should be kept at the incident centre location and in the disaster back-up stores.

Transport and communication lines are established — disaster controller arranges that taxis are standing by and that a communications centre is established — he must ensure that the telephone switchboard operators channel all relevant calls to the incident centre.

Establish second line support groups — once the initial disaster recovery procedures have been initiated then the disaster controller ensures that the following support groups are established:

— software/program maintenance team (including supplier support personnel);
— computer operators;
— data preparation staff;
— paper handling staff;
— disaster salvage team.

Maintaining overall co-ordination and control of events — all information is channelled through the disaster controller — one person must be in control of events.

Disaster assessment procedures

Disaster assessment should be assigned to a member of staff who knows the building well — he may be a member of the building administration department.

Arrange rendezvous with emergency services — before arriving at disaster scene contact should be made with a representative of the emergency services (police) and a meeting place agreed.

Establish staff situation — advise emergency services of numbers and location of personnel in the building concerned.

Establish the extent of disaster — in conjunction with the emergency services, assess the extent of disaster to the building and its contents. A realistic assessment of whether any items can be salvaged should be made and the disaster controller informed accordingly. The fire officer may require information as to the location of the main building services (water, gas, electricity), plans showing their location should be in the appendix to this section of the procedures.

Inform disaster controller — maintain communication link with incident centre — give a situation report as soon as possible. Continue to monitor the situation and handle immediate problems at the disaster scene.

Standby site contact procedures

Contacting the standby site should be the responsibility of a senior member of the central computer operations staff.

Contact standby site(s) — full details of contact procedure should be included in this section of the procedures.

Establish resources available — situation should be explained and the amount of computer time available and when it is available should be established. Establish method of entry to standby site if to be used out of normal working hours.

Check computer configuration — verify that standby site computer meets minimum configuration requirements. Details of minimum requirement should be in the appendix to this section of the procedures. Request aid of standby site personnel — it is useful to have support from someone who knows the site well.

Check supplies of stationery — ensure sufficient supply of listing and console paper is available to meet immediate needs.

Inform disaster controller — ensure that the disaster controller is kept fully briefed of standby arrangements.

Standby site support procedure

Standby site support should be the responsibility of a member of the central computer operations staff.

Establish standby site to be used — the correct standby site must be established to ensure the appropriate software files are made available.

Package items required — obtain the appropriate supplies from the disaster back-up store and make ready for transporting to the standby site. The following items must be securely packaged and clearly identified:

— back-up tape files;
— procedure manuals;
— spare tapes and discs;
— special stationery;
— miscellaneous supplies.

It is advisable that suitable packaging is available in the disaster back-up store to facilitate this task.

Check latest program versions — a check should be made with the programmers to verify if back-up files contain the latest versions of all programs — a new version may have been released immediately prior to or on the night of the disaster.

Inform the disaster controller — indicate transport required to transport back-up supplies to standby site. Transportation may take place in several stages. It is essential that the supplies are transported in the order they are to be used.

Standby site operating procedures

Operating the standby site should be the responsibility of a senior member of the central computer operations staff.

Liaise with standby site personnel — there must be a proper handover of the computer. '

Initialise system to support own requirements — a detailed checklist of action required should be included in the appendix of this section of the procedures.

Restore production files — recreate production files and re-run systems affected by the disaster. The relevant procedures for each application system must be available for this purpose. System recovery procedures are particularly important as your most experienced staff may not be available to carry out the task (so copy all files and secure them).

Complete all control documentation — it is important, particularly in a disaster recovery situation, to ensure all control documentation is completed as normal. Maintain a proper audit trail of the steps in disaster recovery .

Inform disaster controller — Keep the disaster controller informed of the situation at the standby site. Estimates of recovery time need to be established and processing priorities for the production work defined.

Work assessment procedures

Work assessment should be the responsibility of a senior member of the data control staff.

Establish impact of disaster on work schedules — the time of the disaster will be critical in assessing the impact on the work schedules. Effort should initially be concentrated upon the major production systems.

Consult user departments — consult user departments as soon as possible to establish priorities. A list of all user department representatives' names, addresses and telephone numbers should be included in the appendix to this section of the procedures.

Inform disaster controller — advise the disaster controller as soon as possible of the work to be re-run, the run priorities and the resources required. Run times may be longer or shorter depending upon the configuration of the standby computer. Time may have to be allowed for the recreation of input data.

Job preparation — the job documentation and JCL files will need to be prepared for the re-runs and for subsequent processing at the standby site. The establishment of a time-sharing link would be very helpful for this task.

Advise user departments — inform user departments of the revised work schedules and give them some indication of when their work will be completed.

Summary

Reliability, security and control are interconnected themes which demand considerable attention in distributed processing systems.

Here are the main points developed in this chapter:

— design for reliability (using modularity, simplicity, duplication and proven components);
— ensure standby and fall-back systems are available in the event of failure;
— design for fast recovery (using checkpoints, transaction logs, batch recovery and audit programs);
— use the checklist of system controls as a design aid and as the focal point of an audit;
— improve system security by identifying the main threats, introducing controls in sensitive areas and enforcing them;
— use the checklist of precautions against physical risks as a basis for installation planning;
— design disaster procedures, train staff in the principles and periodically carry out disaster tests (say every year test one complete system).

11 Operational running

Most organisations moving to distributed processing already have an experienced central operations team. Although this experience has traditionally been locked into the central site, there is much to be gained by involving central operations with local minicomputers. First, the job is likely to be done better and secondly the operations team will be less threatened by the move to distributed processing — they will be part of it.

When considering the operation of local sites we can identify three main classes of machine:

1. Stand-alone office computer (a simple one-VDU machine);
2. Local computer with no permanent files (maybe an intelligent terminal linked to a central machine);
3. Local computer with permanent files.

The *office computer* is more like an accounting machine in operation than a computer. It should be designed from the start to work with no specialist operators (nobody is called 'the operator'). It is run by clerical staff in the normal course of their duties. The main role of the central staff is to provide support when things go wrong; to manage back-up, consumables and the maintenance of equipment. The local staff should contact central operations first if they have any difficulty rather than the supplier or the projects staff.

The *local computer with no permanent files* should also be designed to run with no specialist operators. File management and file security are the jobs which require an extra degree of specialisation. By running a local computer linked to files at the centre, the cost may be higher (in terms of communications) but the requirement for local operating skills is reduced.

The role of the central operations staff is to provide the file management in a way which is transparent to the local clerical staff. Once again the local staff should contact central operations first if they have any problems — operations solve the problem themselves or call in the right specialist. For example, if a link is involved, central operations should provide on-line diagnostic aids for terminal equipment, lines and modems and should co-ordinate maintenance activities of external suppliers.

The *local computer with permanent files* requires a significantly higher degree of operating skills than do the first two examples. And there is a further problem. The skills are only required when things go wrong. When all is going well the level of competence can be reduced (otherwise the operator is bored with too little to do). There is no easy way out of this dilemma — particularly at remote sites where getting support staff quickly may not be possible. The ideal solution is for the user staff to operate the computer in normal conditions and for operations staff to provide:

— operating standards and procedures;
— back-up when things go wrong;
— operators for late working.

The user staff members are selected for their steadiness under pressure (rather than brilliance) and are trained to follow the procedures and to report accurately and completely whenever anything goes wrong. Central operations can help to select appropriate staff and should have suitable aptitude tests available.

It will be tempting for such user staff to start learning how to program the local machine. Such a trend is a fact which cannot be resisted. Their work should be restricted, however, to time-sharing type jobs (stand-alone) and statistics. All their programming should be to departmental standards and under no circumstances should they be allowed to touch mainfiles (for accounting security) or program suites (how can they then be maintained?).

Systems/operations interface

The point has already been made that once the new system is in operation the ongoing relationship should be between the users and operations. This is in contrast to the development phase of the project where most of the communication is between the project team and the users.

It is thus the responsibility of the project manager to involve operations management in the development and to withdraw after live running. Otherwise the user will always be calling back the projects staff for assistance and not allowing them to get on with the next job.

There are other good reasons for involving operations staff early:

— even well-intentioned analysts have blind spots and tend to overlook operational constraints, the impact of this project on others, the problems of file management, restart and recovery;
— installing equipment is frustrating and intermittently time-consuming. It can get too little attention until suddenly it is on the critical path;
— setting installation standards and writing operating procedures requires knowledge and also time.

These are all areas where the operations experts can be of material assistance to get the project off to a smooth start. In practice operations involvement depends on the nature of the project and the project stage. The guidelines are described in the next few pages.

Survey stage

We can identify five main 'players' in any project:

— user managers, who have the final say in what will be done;
— user staff, who have to operate the new system;
— project team of manager, analysts and programmers who are introducing change;
— operations management, who set the operating standards;
— operations staff, who run the batch jobs on the computers and service on-line jobs.

In the survey stage the relationships are as shown in Figure 11.1.

The project team (P) are finding out what happens from user staff (US) and testing ideas on the user management (UM). They may well also be screening hardware solutions. As a minimum standard the operations management (OM) should be supplied with:

— a copy of the project brief;
— a copy of the survey report at least a week before it will be circulated to users.

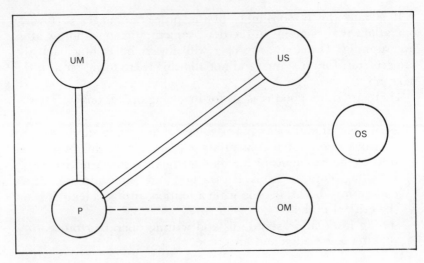

Figure 11.1 Survey stage relationships

If the project is at all complex or interacts with other systems, the systems designer would be well advised to involve his operations counterpart to a far greater extent than the minimum suggested.

Evaluation stage

The evaluation stage is where the Functional Description is prepared (which defines the business need) and where the technical Design Strategy is finalised. The relationships now are illustrated in Figure 11.2.

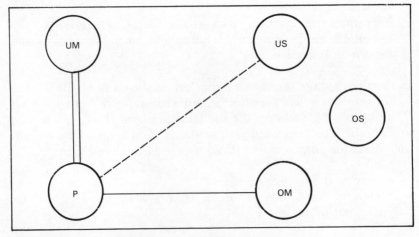

Figure 11.2 Evaluation stage relationships

Operations management should be involved in all discussions on computer operational running in the same way as the user management is involved in finalising the way the business need will be satisfied. Particular issues for operations include:

— hardware requirements and back-up;
— interfaces with existing systems;
— projected running times, housekeeping times;
— projected staffing levels;
— staffing methods (particularly remote sites);
— teleprocessing requirements;
— security, control and recovery methods.

As a minimum standard, operations management must get a copy of the functional description and design strategy one week before they are issued to user management.

Once the evaluation report has been accepted, and decisions taken on the system solution and the equipment required to support it, it is the responsibility of operations to:

— place equipment orders, including telecommunications;
— progress chase orders to hit deadlines;
— negotiate maintenance contracts;
— keep the project manager informed at least monthly of all developments, particularly problems and how they are being resolved.

Equipment procurement needs to be centralised (otherwise nobody knows what is going on) but cannot be treated as a mere administrative function. It falls neatly into the skills which exist in the central operations team.

Specification stage

In the specification stage, operations management are treated in the same way as the users. They have to sign off those parts of the specification that concern them, particularly:

— file security, journalising, saves;
— file recovery;
— file management, volumes, reorganisation;
— file controls.

The relationships are as shown in Figure 11.3.

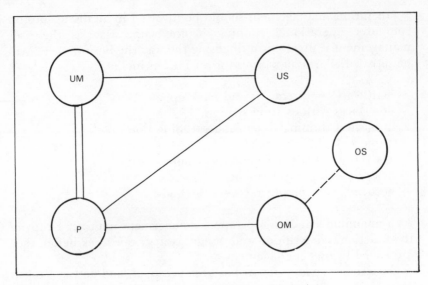

Figure 11.3   Specification stage relationships

It is during the specification stage that the full operational details are established. The systems designer agrees, for every systems specification, details of expected computer throughput:

— input times and methods;
— processing performance;
— impact on other systems;
— output methods and deadlines.

He is verifying the estimates prepared during the Functional Description as a formal activity. Operations management should plan particularly for the way remote sites transmit their input, receive their output and the sequence in which they are processed.

Implementation stage

The implementation stage starts for the operations team immediately after the decision to go ahead (at the end of the evaluation stage). It is during this stage that operational standards and procedures are set up for the needs of the particular user, machine and system under development. The relationships are now at their most complex (Figure 11.4) and it is up to the project manager to ensure good communications — in particular to get user management and operations management together. Between them they can take much of the strain.

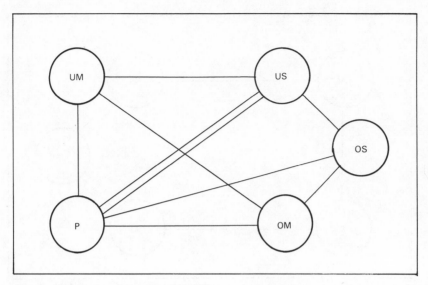

Figure 11.4 Implementation stage relationships

On any significant project a senior member of the operations department will be seconded to the project team on a full-time basis. The jobs to be done include:

— supervising the site survey and site preparation;
— supervising machine installation and commissioning;
— operational standards and procedures;
— operator training and post-implementation support.

Carrying out these time-consuming jobs is of material help to the project manager who would otherwise be in danger of getting diverted from the mainstream of his project. To ensure good communication, a member of operations management should sit on the implementation steering committee whenever operations activities appear on the project bar-chart — at other times he should be copied with implementation committee minutes.

By the time live running has been reached the relationships have moved to centre on the user staff and operations staff — and hopefully the projects staff are down to amendments and helping in a knotty crisis.

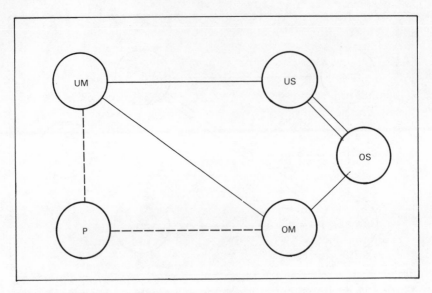

Figure 11.5 Live running relationships

Site preparation

Once a decision has been taken to place new hardware in a new or existing site the operations representative carries out a site survey for the user management with the hardware supplier. They must establish:

— a suitable location (there may be implications for a number of departments in the building);
— power requirements (and getting a clean supply) — which may involve a working knowledge of international power supply differences;
— layout of equipment (with the hardware supplier);
— telecommunications requirements (with the PTT);
— environmental requirements (air conditioning);
— physical security requirements;
— engineers' space requirements;
— computer staffing levels (and working hours);
— media and stationery requirements.

As a minimum requirement the site survey report should be discussed with the project manager one week before issue to the users.

Once the plan is agreed, external contractors (electricians, builders, plumbers, etc.) can be contacted, costs agreed and work commenced. An established administration department may well carry out the detailed ordering but the operations representative is responsible for supervising:

— installation of power supplies;
— building of computer room and ancillary areas;
— installation and testing of environmental controls.

The machine area is now ready for the installation of the machine and the operations representative carries out the following tasks:

— supervising the installation of the computer and ancillary equipment;
— carrying out hardware/software commissioning tests;
— preparing machine commissioning report;
— ensuring manufacturers' manuals are supplied;
— setting up regular preventive maintenance routines;
— keeping the project manager informed of all problems.

The time involved in all these activities will depend on the complexity of the installation (from a micro with a 13 amp plug to a full mainframe complex). Generous time allowances need to be made for suppliers to miss delivery dates, for equipment not to work or for the wrong equipment to be delivered.

Commissioning hardware, for example, involves carrying out extensive tests on every component of the machine (printers working continuously for two hours with printing, spacing and skipping; disc reorganisation with continuous head movement for four hours). The commissioning engineer is likely to regard this sort of testing as abuse of the machine. But it is very necessary to iron out all the problems before it is handed over to the project team and users.

Operating standards and procedures

The systems analysts on the team prepare the user manuals and similarly the operations representative prepares operating procedures. Typical section headings are:

INTRODUCTION
— Hardware description
— System description

— Running times
— Program running
— System usage
— Hardware maintenance — engineer liaison
— Software maintenance

COMPUTER ROOM PROCEDURES
— Hardware operation
— Software start up/shut down
— Tape and disc library procedures
— Error logging, recovery and reporting
— Security
— Computer room maintenance
— Ordering supplies
— Controlling program releases and versions
— Back-up procedures
— Scheduling and JCL

RUNNING SUPERVISORY PROGRAMS
— Start-of-day procedures
— Run control and error recovery
— End-of-day procedures
— System utilities

RUNNING APPLICATION PROGRAMS
— System flowchart and run timings
— Program operating instructions
— Output distribution procedures and deadlines
— File reorganisation
— Special recovery procedures

As each section of the manual is completed it should be passed to the project manager so that the project team can comment on and agree the contents.

Training and post-implementation support

Once the machine has been installed and the operating procedures prepared, the operations representative will train all relevant staff in:

— hardware/software operation;
— application program running (computer end);
— operating standards and procedures.

He then supervises live running until confident that the staff are competent. His involvement gradually decreases but never stops altogether — even if the users are running their own equipment. He should set up periodic progress meetings (not more than one a month and not fewer than two a year) with the user management to review the way the system is running.

In practice the operations representative may carry out a number of additional tasks to help the project team — depending on pressures at the time. He may well be able to assist with system and acceptance testing, file conversion/creation and in parallel running.

Members of the project team, after working closely with the users to develop the system, will receive many of the user comments and complaints about the system. These comments should be directed towards the operations representative who will then have the chance to improve any operational failings. The project team should resist the temptation to solve all the problems themselves — they will never get on to the next project otherwise.

Some systems give continual problems in operation while others run smoothly and successfully. In both cases the operations management should communicate with the projects management so that they may profit from the lessons learned. Clearly this is a sensitive area, as nobody likes to be criticised but the overall goal is to produce first-class systems using the best experience available.

Summary

The operations interface in many ways is as important as the user interface. It is, however, easily overlooked. Involving operations management early enough will help project development and ensure a smooth transition to live running.

12 Controlling systems development

This book is about *designing* a distributed processing system. It has concentrated on only one, very important aspect of the whole project. If the project is to be successful the right relations have to be built up with the users using the right project team.

The author's book *A guide to the successful management of computer projects* has been referenced already. It is a companion book in the sense that it is a *how to* guide. Perhaps the most important points it brings out are:

1. the need for the right project framework:
   — user relations;
   — choice of project and project manager.
2. the need for a practical control mechanism:
   — five-stage approach to project development.

We conclude this book by summarising these points which have been there by implication through all the discussion.

Structuring project responsibilities

A computer system is not an end in itself. It only exists to support a business need. It follows that the line manager who is going to run the system must be involved in the design — in fact more than involved; committed to its success. The reporting structure found to be most successful is shown in Figure 12.1.

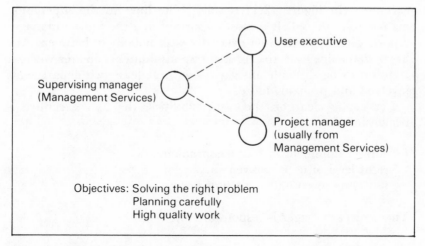

Figure 12.1   Project organisation

The user executive is a key appointment. He should be at director level and have line responsibility for the ongoing business system. His role is not full-time and he will delegate day-to-day involvement to members of his staff. He has, however, overall responsibility for the project, for ensuring that the business needs are correctly stated, and that the user department wholeheartedly support the new system. **If a suitable user executive cannot be found the project should be stopped.** If nobody will sponsor it at this stage they are even less likely to later on when the going gets tough (as it does).

The project manager is the full-time leader of the project. To be successful he needs to have a good technical knowledge, a sound business knowledge and be good at project management. Usually he is supplied by management services and it is up to the user executive to ensure that any gaps in his business understanding are remedied.

However good the project manager, he always benefits from a second opinion. The job of the supervising manager is to provide such a second opinion. He has a relationship with both the user executive and the project manager that allows him to counsel in three specific areas:

— solving the right problem (has a greater understanding caused a shift in requirement?);
— assisting with project planning (planning to avoid problems);
— ensuring high-quality work (to agreed standards of performance).

Notice that the line joining the project manager to the user executive (in Figure 12.1) is solid. The lines to the supervising manager are dotted. It is most important that the project manager reports directly to the user executive with nobody in between. Any break in the line leads to confused responsibilities in an area where it is going to be difficult anyway — with at least two departments involved and probably more.

Let us be clear on the responsibilities: the user executive is responsible for:

— correct statement of business problem;
— right level of user involvement;
— satisfying, eventually, the user needs.

The project manager is responsible for:

— day-to-day running of the project;
— all staff working on the project;
— meeting time, cost and quality objectives.

The supervising manager is responsible for:

— quality control;
— providing a second opinion;
— obtaining resources.

Choosing the project manager

'Good management' in any sphere of activity seems to have three ingredients:

— *technical ability,* enough to be able to judge the quality of the work of subordinates;
— *leadership ability,* a desire and ability to get results;
— *conceptual thinking ability,* able to take an objective stance, one step removed from the immediate problem.

Let us use this classification to see what qualities are required in our project manager.

During the initial creative phase, technical ability means having a depth understanding of the business problem together with a good understanding of systems solutions. Leadership ability is not project team management but handling user directors and staff; the ability to disagree constructively. Conceptual thinking ability is a vital ingredient if a good solution is to be found; the problem needs to be studied as one of a class of problems, anticipating growth and change.

During the execution phase of the project the emphasis shifts. Technical ability means not only a sound computer knowledge but also an awareness of people and systems — the human interface and what can be achieved with a computer system. Leadership ability means giving out the right size tasks and checking that they get done; a systematic recording of all agreements and meticulous attention to detail. Conceptual thinking ability is shown in the desire to look ahead, avoiding problems by forward planning. It is not often that all these qualities are found in one man; but if we are aware that they are needed we can build a more balanced management team. A project manager whose strength is attention to detail might best be supported by an experienced supervising manager who is good at forward planning.

Of all the qualities, giving out the right size tasks and then checking that they get done is the one to prize most highly in a project manager. The attribute to avoid is lack of success. In this business people do not seem to learn by their mistakes (at least not in a global sense). The qualities that caused the problems on the first project will emerge again in the stress of the second — in spite of temporary reforms. So do not pander to your instinctive sense of fair play by giving him a second chance; give him a different job which he can do well and get another project manager. It is more realistic, and kinder.

So far we have assumed that the right person for the job is available from somewhere within the organisation — in practice it is often not the case. There are certain skills which *must* be available — experienced business analyst, system designer, system programmer, implementation manager. The absence of such expert advice almost guarantees problems on the project, so the skill will have to be hired if it has not yet been developed. Nevertheless the bulk of the work can be done by less experienced staff — provided they have the aptitude and provided they are correctly supervised. If you know there are weak links the safeguard is to have more frequent reviews. You may even find that the projects with less experienced staff, but with this tighter quality control, do rather better than projects with more experienced staff where quality is taken for granted.

Stages of system development

Identifying project activities correctly is probably the most important part of project management. To make it easier we start by recognising that a project goes through a number of *stages*. The five stages of project development are illustrated in Figure 12.2.

Survey stage

The end result of the survey stage is the survey report. This report is concerned primarily with 'what is the problem to be solved?'. Its main headings are thus:

— current situation;
— requirements of new/improved system;
— alternative solutions considered;
— evaluation of alternatives;
— recommended approach.

There is a risk that considering alternatives (solutions) too early will cloud the problem statement but equally the bit of the problem that is worth solving may depend on the solution selected. If necessary the report can be in two parts which separate the 'what' from the 'how'.

Evaluation stage

In the evaluation stage the proposed solution is examined in depth and two documents are prepared. The first is the functional description and the second contains the design strategy. One is the detailed business statement, the other is the detailed technical realisation. The main headings in the functional description are:

— system overview;
— narrative description of every business procedure;
— specimen outputs;
— specimen inputs;
— summary of main file contents;
— tabulation of codes;
— control principles;
— volumes, file sizes and run timings;
— user responsibilities;
— implementation plan and costs.

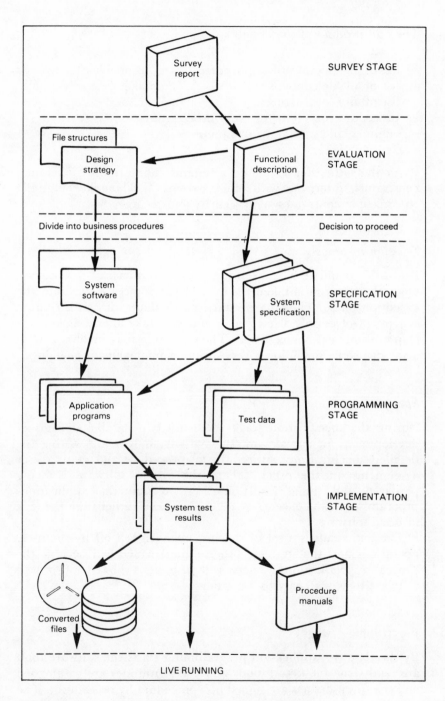

Figure 12.2   The stages of system development

The end product of the design strategy is:

— list of all files and their purpose;
— list of all file contents;
— list of all file structures;
— procedure run chart for every procedure;
— volumes, file sizes and run timings.

Particular attention is paid to systems 'blind spots' — timing constraints, interfaces with other systems, file housekeeping, file copying, file controls, system security and recovery.

Decision to proceed

Up to this point we have been in the creative phase of the project. Once the decision is taken to proceed the project moves into the execution phase. The creative start, particularly with a distributed system, involves only a few people but may take almost as long (in elapsed time) as the execution. The execution may involve a small army of people providing a very different management challenge.

Specification stage

During the specification stage there are two parallel streams of development. In one stream, the systems analysts are writing the detailed specifications, procedure by procedure and getting user agreement. In the other stream the system software is being prepared and tested (tool building) so that the applications programmers can concentrate on the problem rather than the lack of basic software.

The end result is a set of specifications (signed off by the user, operations and the strategic programmer) which will become the program specifications. There will also be a library of proven software tools with easy-to-use guides.

Programming stage

By the time the application programming starts the software tools are ready, the file descriptions and access routines are catalogued and the specifications are signed off (procedure by procedure). The programmers are thus free to get on and solve the business problem. The job of the programmer is to:

— study the systems specification;
— structure his programs clearly;
— write the code;
— carry out program testing;
— complete program documentation.

To assist the process he is given program 'skeletons' of the major program types (particularly match/merge/update). The strategic programmer has the job of reviewing program structures and program link testing.

In parallel with programming, the analysts are systematically preparing system test data which will independently test the program suites.

Implementation stage

Although the implementation stage is logically the fifth stage of project development many of the activities commence immediately following the decision to proceed. Here are the implementation acitivites:
— system and acceptance testing;
— manual procedures;
— operating procedures;
— equipment procurement and external factors;
— interfaces with related systems;
— file conversion;
— holding point and audit approval;
— user organisation and training;
— parallel running and going live;
— old system shutdown;
— post-implementation support.

These activities can all be quite substantial and require a high degree of co-ordination from the project manager.

Management style

Good project management is easy to recognise. Here are the cardinal rules:

1. *Structure the problem to be solved* so that it is reduced to manageable activities. This structuring requires technical competence to ensure that the interaction within the activity greatly exceeds the interaction between activities.
2. *Plan ahead* so that jobs are done in a sensible sequence. Aim to identify and remove all bottlenecks and obstacles to smooth progress.
3. *Give clear instructions* on the job to be done, the expected results and the time-scale allowed.
4. *Provide a quality control framework* so that staff know the standard expected of them. If there exists a published 'best way' of doing a job it is easier for staff to identify where they are deviating from standard and to justify it if appropriate.
5. *Ensure the job is within the competence of the individual concerned.* Does he have the skill and the training required? Does the size of the job measure up to his level of experience?
6. *Delegate the work* by allowing team members to get on with the job without fussy supervision. After all you have created a working framework which makes it possible.
7. *Control performance* in terms of quality and time. Tell the staff what is expected of them and tell them how they are performing. Act on deviations.
8. *Give public recognition* for good work well done. We all like to make a visible contribution to the work of a group and to have our contribution recognised.

These are the rules of good *project* management. They are also good rules for management in any sphere.

Select bibliography

Chapter 1 & 2

Down, P.J. and Taylor, F.E., *Why Distributed Computing?* National Computing Centre (NCC), UK.

Champine, G.A., *Computer Technology Impact on Management.* North Holland Publishing Co.

Chapter 3

Chang, S.K., *A Model for Distributed Computer System Design.* IEEE Trans SMC-5 no.6 pp.344-359 (1976).

Severino, E.F., *Databases and Distributed Processing.* Computer Decisions vol.9 no.3 (1977).

Chapter 4

Telecommunications, IBM Systems Journal vol.18 no.2 (1979).

UK Post Office, *Handbook of Data Communications,* NCC.

Chapter 5

Palmer, I.R., *Practicalities in applying a formal methodology to data analysis*, CACI.

Martin, J., *Computer Data-base Organisation*, Prentice-Hall.

Chapter 6

Bell, C.G., Mudge, J.C., McNamara, J.E., *Computer Engineering — a DEC view of hardware systems design*, Digital Press (1978).

Barron, D., *Operating Systems*, MacDonald.

Mahmoud, S.A. and Toth, K.C., *A modelling approach to systems analysis of processing networks*, Canadian Datasystems, vol.9, no.3 (1977).

Chapter 7

Cakir, A., Hart, D., Steward, T., *The VDT Manual*, IFRA, West Germany.

Workstations, ADP Newsletter, vol.20, no.19 (1976).

Martin, J., *Real Time Dialogue Design*, Addison-Wesley.

Chapter 8

Jackson, M., *Principles of Program Design*, Academic Press.

Spier, M.J., *Software Malpractice — a distasteful experience*. Software — Practice and Experience, vol.6, no.3 (1976).

Chapter 9

Martin, J., *Systems Analysis for Data Transmission*, Prentice-Hall.

Bard, Y., *An Analytic Model of the VM/370 System*. IBM Journal of Research and Development, vol.22, no.5 (1978).

Chapter 10

Pritchard, J.A.T., *Quantitative Methods in On-line Systems* (Part 4). NCC.

Chapter 11

Green, R., *Using minicomputers in Distributed Systems*. NCC.

Shepherd, A.J., *A British Example of Distributed Computing*, Datamation, vol.24, no.3 (1978).

Chapter 12

Donaldson, H., *A Guide to the Successful Management of Computer Projects*. Associated Business Press (UK); Halstead Press (USA).

Lehman, J.H., *How Software Projects are Really Managed*. Datamation, vol.25, no.1.

Index

access to centralised data, 79
accommodation costs, 8
acoustic coupler, 63
application packages, 124, 165
arrival distribution from random
   numbers, 183
ASCII character set, 59
assembly language, 122
asymmetrical duplex, 63
asynchronous transmission, 57, 70

back-up systems, 186
BASIC, 123
BASIC program, 180
basic software, summary of, 122
basic utilities, 120
batch input, 32
batch system, 10
binary synchronous transmission, 56
bit stuffing, 74
block check character, 55
block lockout, 87
bottleneck areas, 182
B-tree organisation, 98, 99
business culture, 50
business needs, 16, 23

cache memory, 109
central approach, 78
centralisation, 16
centralised files, 45

chained file organisation, 104
chained transactions, 105
character stuffing, 57
checklist of main files, 47
circuit switching, 72
COBOL, 123
codes, 32
communications networks, 54
communicatins, 2780 point-to-point,
   54, 55
computer architecture, 14
computer investment, 50
computer operations costs, 4
concentrators, 67
control, 185
control characters, 56
control codes, 137
cost/benefit analysis, 169
costs, accommodation, 8
costs, data input, 10
costs, data transmission, 8
costs, hardware, 6
costs, hardware maintenance, 8
costs, staff, 6, 7
cost trends, 4, 9, 12, 13
cost trends analysis, 11
CPU capacity, 183
current loop interface, 60
custom-built hardware, 124
custom peripherals, 125
cyclic redundancy check, 55, 74

Dartmouth system, 118
data analysis, 88
database management systems
   (DBMS), 104
data entry screen design, 139
data files, location of, 40
data input costs, 10
data link escape (DLE), 57
data transmission costs, 8
data transparency, 74
deadlock, 84
decision support systems, 29
decision to proceed, 224
design approach, 27
designing on-line systems, 153
design rules, 17
digital switching, 71
direct memory access (DMA), 110
disaster control procedures, 200
distributed applications, 80
distributed files, 45, 77
duplex, 63

EIA interface, 59
enquiry screen design, 143
erasable programmable read only
   memory (EPROM), 114
Erlang distribution, 173
evaluation stage, 210, 222
eyestrain, 133

fall-back methods, 187
field handling, 162
file access methods, 77, 94, 105
file contents, 26
file design, 88
file handling, 162
file location guidelines, 49
file lockout, 82
file management requirements, 121
file organisation methods, 95
file ownership, 47
file strategy, 26, 40
file strategy guidelines, 45
file structure decisions, 92
Fintel, 144, 146, 147
foreground/background real-time
   systems, 116
formatted screens, 139, 141, 142
frequency division multiplexing, 63
front end processors, 66, 109
full duplex, 63

functional packages, 124, 165
function keys, 135

half duplex, 63
hardware, choice of, 127
hardware costs, 6
hardware maintenance costs, 8
hardware overview, 107
hardware strategy, 107
hashing algorithm, 101
hash random methods, 98
hierarchical approach v. stand-alone
   approach, 46
hierarchical computer organisation, 41
hierarchical network, 19
high level data link control (HDLC),
   74
high level language, 123

IBM Series 1 architecture, 112
implementation stage, 212, 213, 225
implementation timescale, 169
indexed access method (IAM), 98
index sequential access method
   (ISAM), 93, 95, 96, 97
information flow, constraints of, 42
input/output multiplexer, 109
intelligent terminals, 70
interactive databases, 78
interleaved memory, 109
interrupt vector, 111
inverted files, 103
investment management company case
   study, 35

keyboard, 126
keying and transmission times, table
   of, 177

levels of communication, 75
lighting, 130
line capacity, 182
line concentration, 69
line conditioning, 56
live running relationships, 214
local economies of scale, 51
local stand-alone approach, 81
loction of data files, 40
longitudinal redundancy check, 55
long line drivers, 125
look ahead technique, 109

mainframe architecture, 108
mainframe approach, 18
mainframe computer, definition of, 107
mainframe operating systems, 115
mainframe operators, 5
mainframe software overhead, 117
management information hierarchy, 29
management information require-ments, 28
management style, 225
management view of distributed processing, 2
memory capacity, 183
message switching, 71, 80
microcomputer architecture, 112, 113
microcomputers, definition of, 108
minicomputer operating systems, 116, 117
minicomputers, architecture, 110
minicomputers, definition of, 107
modem, 56
modularity of design, 186
multiple update protection, 82
multiplexer, 63
multipoint line, 66, 67
multi-user real-time operating systems, 118

office environment, 130
on-line input, 157
on-line program design, 153
on-line system recovery, 190
on-line systems, 11
on-line systems, impact on business organisation, 30
on-line systems, design of, 153
open order file organisation, 91
operating environment improvements, 126
operating needs, 24, 25
operating standards and procedures, 215
operating system requirements, 120
operating systems, overview, 114
operational control, 28, 30
operational running, 207
organisational constraints, 50
organisational implications, 32
organisation structure, 37

package approach, 25
packages, 124, 164, 165
packages, choice of, 166
package testing, 168
packet switching, 72, 73
page lockout, 84
parallelism, 184
patchboard, 126
paterns of decisions, 30
payroll system, 159
performance characteristics, 171
peripheral handling, 163
physical risks, precautions against, 198
polling, 67
post-implementation support, 216
Prestel, 144
preventive maintenance, 188
prime numbers, table of, 100
privacy, 196
private networks, 71
privileged account, 148
product codes, 34
product master file checklist, 33
programmable read only memory (PROM), 126
programming conventions, 164
programming language, choice of, 121
programming stage, 224
programming strategy, 153
program skeletons, 164, 225
program suites, 157
project manager, choice of, 220
project organisation, 219
project responsibilities, 218
protocol levels, 74
pseudo real-time updating, 156, 193
public networks, 71
purchase ledger system, 160

question and answer mode, 139, 140
queuing principles, 172
queuing system, 171

random access, 31, 93
random access memory (RAM), 114, 126
random files, 95
randomising algorithm, 100, 102
read only memory (ROM), 114
real-time system recovery, 192
real-time updating, 154, 155, 191
record chaining, 104
record lockout, 82, 85

relative organisation, 95
relaxation allowance, 133
reliability, 195
reliability checklist, 188
remote job entry (RJE), 54
report generators, 143
restricted access, 149
risks, precautions against, 198
risks, reducing, 26, 52

schema, 105
screen design, 135, 138
security, 185, 196
security of access, 144
sequential access, 31, 93
sequential organisation, 95
simultaneous update, 83
site preparation, 214
software, 118, 163
software functions, 161, 163
special purpose terminls, 150
specification stage, 211, 212, 224
speed of response, 48
splitting files by timescale, 49
staff costs, 6, 7
stages of system development, 223
stand-alone approach, 18, 21
standard packages, 164
strategic planning, 28
sub-schema, 105
survey stage, 209, 210, 222
swapping discs, 125
swapping time, 182
SWIFT, 32
synchronous data link control (SDLC), 74
synchronous transmission, 56, 70
system controls checklist, 194
system recovery, 188
systems development, 218, 222
systems/operations interface, 208
system utilities, 163

tabulated entries, 145
tactical planning, 28

telephone conversation and computer protocol compared, 57
terminal capacity, 182
third normal form (TNF), 89
time division multiplexing, 63, 65
time division switching, 73
timesharing systems, 116
timesharing system commands, 119
top down data transfer, 20
training and post-implementation support, 216
training and supervision, 149
transaction files, structuring, 31
transaction processing, 81
transmission failure, 189
transmission speeds, 43
transparent mode transmission, 56
tree search routines, 144

Unibus, 110
user executive, 150, 219, 220
user manuals, 215
user requirements, 27
users, 26, 36, 119, 134, 136, 149, 150, 204-17

value-added networks, 71
VDU features, 136
VDU input, 32
VDU keyboard, 126
VDU screen esign, 135, 138
VDU, interactive, 61
VDUs, siting, 34
VDU time, 143
VDU workflow, 35
virtual circuit, 73
virtual terminal, 75
voice grade lines, 56
volume of transactions, 48

workflow, 134
workflow design, 129
working measurements, 133
work posture, 131